HILLTOP SCHOOLS
South Defiance Street
West Unity, Ohio 43570

PATHWAYS TO PROSPERITY

330
Wil

BORROWER'S CARD
Wilson, Kenneth

Pathways to Prosperity School Library

330
Wil

Pathways to Prosperity

CHOICES FOR SUCCESS IN THE INFORMATION AGE

Kenneth D. Wilson
Richard Goldhurst

PRAEGER

PRAEGER SPECIAL STUDIES • PRAEGER SCIENTIFIC

Library of Congress Cataloging in Publication Data

Wilson, Kenneth D.
  Pathways to prosperity.

  Includes index.
  1. United States—Economic policy—1981–
  2. Energy policy—United States. I. Goldhurst, Richard.
  II. Title.
  HC106.8.W56   1983   338.973   83-11177
  ISBN 0-03-069538-4 (alk. paper)

Published in 1983 by Praeger Publishers
CBS Educational and Professional Publishing
a Division of CBS Inc.
521 Fifth Avenue, New York, NY 10175 USA
© by Kenneth D. Wilson and Richard Goldhurst

All rights reserved

456789 052 98765432

Printed in the United States of America
on acid-free paper

Foreword

From an international or even national perspective, economic and energy policy issues are extremely complex and elusive. It is difficult to grasp the fluid interplay of social, political, economic, and technological factors and even harder to visualize billions of dollars or quadrillions of British thermal units (Btus). Most people deal with these matters only in the personal choices they make. Do they save or spend? Do they drive to work or ride the bus?

Individual choices, added up, produce the national statistics so large they become abstractions. Many books take on the economic and energy supply problems at the national level. That is indeed a valuable perspective. But ultimately everything comes down to human and personal choices.

In this book the "big picture" is presented as background for the real actors in the economy—people living their lives. Chapter 1 discusses the national perspective, as a stage setting helping us to get oriented and providing a basis for charting the right course. Chapter 2 assesses the problems and challenges to be overcome (we call them Navigational Hazards).

Chapter 3 lays out a preferred path, first in terms of a national economic scenario and then as a narrative of the lives and choices of some fictional U.S. citizens. Chapter 4 translates the preferred scenario and individual choices into public policy recommendations.

Chapter 5 presents profiles of ten real people who are models for achieving prosperity in the broadest sense. People are our country's ultimate resource. Most of the book is devoted to the success stories of these people because they and others like them are the nation's real wealth.

Although these ten individuals come from diverse backgrounds, each illustrates qualities necessary to achieve the preferred path. The overall pattern of their lives is one of openness to changing conditions—an attitude of experimentation and a willingness to be surprised. These people have a high tolerance for uncertainty and the capacity to accept risks. They are not committed to maintaining the status quo, nor do they avoid hard work. Each demonstrates perseverance and strength of will arising out of a commitment to a larger goal or greater good coupled with a belief in a positive outcome. They are dedicated to community service and rely on cooperation to resolve conflict. These are pragmatic individuals, but they do not settle for short-term expedient solutions. As a group these models are a source of inspiration for this book, which is itself motivated by a positive vision of the future.

Chapter 6 weaves together the life patterns of the models with the characteristics of the preferred economic scenario. Overall, the message of this book is one of optimism at a time when people have doubts and fears about their nation's and their own future. Our society is passing from one economic and energy era to another along an unmarked trail and with an uncertain destination. We meet roadblocks and detours along the route, but we also know that there are ways through. When one era ends, a new one begins. Of the many different futures that are possible, this book points out *Pathways to Prosperity*.

Acknowledgments

The authors wish to acknowledge the editorial contributions made to this book by Norm Rubinstein in Washington, D.C., and Nancy Bryan in Los Angeles. Bill Thompson in Philadelphia provided valuable assistance. Special appreciation is expressed to Kathy Allen, Joanne Camacho, and Pam Romero who provided word-processing services through many drafts of the manuscript.

This volume benefited from the careful reading, critical comments, and suggestions of colleagues, friends, and family members who are greatly appreciated. Any errors are the responsibility of the authors.

Contents

		Page
FOREWORD		v
ACKNOWLEDGMENTS		vii

Chapter

1 CHARTING A COURSE   1

    Approaching the Future with a Ten-Foot Pole   1
    Focusing on a Goal   3
    The True Meaning of Survival and Prosperity   5

2 NAVIGATIONAL HAZARDS   7

    The Economy at Low Tide   7
    Energy: A Shifting Current   10
    Other Resources: Soil and Water   11
    Environmental Challenges   13
    Entropy: The Threat of Winding Down   15
    Nuclear War: The Ultimate Hazard   16
    Who Is at the Wheel?   18

3 A PREFERRED PATH   21

    Building a Scenario   21
    GNP—The Foundation   25
    Population Trends   27
    The Impact of Immigration   27
    Work Defines the Community   28
    Productivity for Robinson Crusoe—For You and Me   31
    But We Will Still Pay Taxes   36
    Enter Energy   36

	Living on the Preferred Path	38
	Looking Both Ways	47
4	**POLICY CHOICES FOR THE INFORMATION AGE**	49
	The Information Economy	50
	Productivity and Work	55
	Labor Pains	57
	Rethinking Education	57
	The Positive Role of Government	59
	Policy Choices to Promote Saving and Investment	60
	Controlling Government Spending	61
	Government Spending Targets	63
	Public Capital Investment	63
	Reducing the National Debt	65
	Individual Responsibility versus Government Regulation	65
	Energy: Range of Options	67
	Resolving the Threat of Nuclear War	70
5	**MODELS FOR A PREFERRED PATH TO PROSPERITY**	75
	Jack Horton	76
	Bill Gould	81
	Jim Roseboro	88
	Robert Georgine	91
	Norm King	96
	Josie Bain	103
	Charles Peters, Jr.	109
	Andy Lipkis	113
	Elizabeth Tappe	118
	Ian McMillan	120
	Good Players Make Great Music	125
6	**COMPLETING THE LOG**	127
	Diversity	128
	Productivity and Risk	128
	Openness to Change	129
	Commitment to a Larger Goal	131
	Dedication to Community and Service	133

Cooperation	133
Work and Perseverance	134
Choice over Chance	135

BIBLIOGRAPHY 139

INDEX 143

ABOUT THE AUTHORS 148

1
Charting a Course

A nation, like an individual, must make decisions—decisions that will influence its course for years to come. Over the next 20 years, any number of different economic futures await U.S. citizens depending on which path the country chooses to follow. But two things are common to all possible futures: the role and responsibility every U.S. citizen bears in the economic and political decision-making process, and the importance of the resource and environmental factors outside of human control.

If we are attentive students of our own history, we discover that prosperity has been the result of decisions to pursue economic growth, coupled with the good fortune of abundant resources. When the economy has grown, so has national morale. This book outlines national and individual choices that expand options for economic growth while considering the best use of resources and the environment; in this way the book illustrates directions that could lead to greater national prosperity.

APPROACHING THE FUTURE WITH A TEN-FOOT POLE

Charting a course for the future requires a clear set of goals coupled with a sense of humility and a grain of humor. In all honesty the pace of change today makes it impossible to predict the future. Economists are on a par with weatherforecasters when it comes to predicting future events: both do pretty well when not much is happening. Afterall, when nothing is happening it is very easy to predict it. Fortunately or unfortunately, depending on one's point of view, we living in a time when a great deal is happening. Nevertheless we are bound by a dilemma of the human condition—all of our decisions concern the future, but all of our experience comes from the past. The philosopher Auguste Comte observed in his book *The Positive Philosophy*, "Short as is our life, and feeble as is our reason, we cannot emancipate ourselves from the influence of our environment. Even the wildest dreamers reflect in their dreams the contemporary social state: and much more impossible is it to form a conception of a true political system, radically different from that amidst which we live. The highest order of minds cannot discern the characteristics of the coming period."*

This book makes no predictions about the coming period, nor does it advance any forecasts. It is said that forecasting is the art of saying what will happen and then explaining why it did not. Forecasts are so often wrong because the future takes its specific form from new principles that cannot be visualized in advance. The truly important and distinctive changes are not technical; they are changes in values, perception, and goals. Such factors are not subject to forecasting.

We intend to present a possible scenario, a story about a set of outcomes that could happen *if* certain choices are made by individuals and the society as a whole. Because it could result in national prosperity, we label the scenario "preferred" and present the requisite choices as recommendations. Thus we enter into the risky realm of giving advice. We do this with the full awareness of the message in one small boy's short essay on Socrates: "Socrates was a Greek philosopher, who went around giving people good advice—they poisoned him!"

Willingness to take risks is a key element of the preferred scenario. Therefore, if the message and the messenger are to be congruent, we

---

*Quoted in Harold Orlans, "The Fragmentation and Cohesion of Society," *The Future of the United States Government—Toward the Year 2000*, ed. Harvey S. Perloff. New York: George Braziller, 1971, p. 59.

must be willing to take risks and make our recommemdations in good faith. We hope that the reader thinks of prosperity as a desirable goal, but we do not automatically assume this. At the outset we will decribe the value of working from a vision and a goal and will review the true meaning of "survival" and "prosperity".

FOCUSING ON A GOAL

Prosperity as a product of rising economic output and personal consumption was an accepted national goal until ten or fifteen years ago. But the last two decades have been marked by sudden and constant change, which has bedeviled both the economy and morale of this country. Such change has brought resistance and dislocation and, in turn, has eroded traditional ideas about what constitutes the "typical" U.S. citizen and about the roles of prosperity and economic growth in our national life.

On V-J Day, the United States was first among countries of the world, measured by its industrial plant, its technological expertise, and its profound commitment to a peaceful future. In the almost 30 years since then, our economic stability and moral conviction has been challenged by the oil embargo and rise of the oil cartel, the demoralization wreaked by the Vietnam War and Watergate, the aggressive competition for markets waged by efficient European and Asian industrial nations, the mounting awareness of environmental costs associated with mass consumption, and high inflation. And these are but a handful of the systemic shocks this country has withstood in the last 30 years. Moreover social change has forced revisions of our sense of a shared national identity.

The homogeneity of the melting pot has given way to the heterogeneity of a society now increasingly conscious of its extraordinary diversity. The United States has, for example, a black population second only in size to Nigeria's. It has influential Protestant, Catholic, and Jewish congregations, and large numbers belong to the evangelical sects. The nation is multilingual. More than 600,000 new companies are created in the United States each year, compared with 93,000 three decades ago. It is not suprising that it grows continually harder to characterized the "typical" citizen. At one point in U.S. history most citizens subscribed to the concept of a "Manifest Destiny", settling North America from the Atlantic to the Pacific

Oceans. Today, the public resists the notion of a common possible destiny, much less a manifest one. The experience of the last 30 years has instilled a sense of fragmentation in U.S. citizens. The social alienation of the 1960s and 1970s threatens to become a self-fulfilling prophecy in the 1980s and 1990s.

The distinction between a nation whose diversity adds up to a melting pot and one that exaggerates ethnic, religious, or sexual differences at the expense of national "wholeness" is crucial. Diversity is a source of tremendous strength when harnessed to common goals. But when the modifier in "black Americans," "Hispanic Americans," "female Americans," or "Catholic Americans" takes precedence over the noun, the possibility of social and cultural unity evaporates. A nation oblivious of a shared cultural identity in time loses faith in itself and the government that tries to represent it.

Lacking a sense of common direction, U.S. citizens perplexedly view their economy and its resource picture as a labyrinth—a maze through which they must travel seeking prosperity and security. Familiar formulas and traditional modes of leadership no longer seem to be working. Applying past expectations and performance measures, many people have become discouraged about the nation's prospects for survival.

In the face of slackening productivity, warring fiscal and monetary policies, and declining investment in the future, many citizens feel dissatisfaction—with their schools, their elected leaders, and their economy, to name just three common complaints. They are disappointed that the United States can no longer dominate international events, control domestic consumer markets, or even manage its own national budget. They tend to be optimistic about their individual personal futures but have little faith that their economy will assist, sustain, or protect them.

And yet clearly citizens *are* the economy, which, put simply, is a system composed of people who produce, consume, and create together. Good morale and a sense of shared purpose bring the many parts of an economy into harmony. As workers, material, time, and money come together, they produce an effect greater than the sum of their parts. The word for this fusion of effort is synergy. Today, the road to economic prosperity and individual and national security is no different than it has ever been: men and women realize a future by envisioning certain goals and by inspiring others to help bring them about. The early Congresses of the United States facilitated the settlement of the uncertain frontier by making the first stages of Manifest Destiny a shared national goal in which U.S. citizens felt a vested interest. Revolutionary War veterans were paid with land west of the Smokies, the United States Military Academy was established to provide engineers for the frontier, and pioneers were promised representation when the population in the new territories reached certain levels.

Defining a goal, however, did not and still does not insure absolute control. Plans are modified by chance, by good or bad luck. On one hand, the movement west was slowed by diseases, adverse weather, and the fear (and reality) of attack; on the other, the gold in Sutter's Creek speeded the western settlement past expectation. What do we learn from our experience? The future is not fated nor is it sheer happenstance. It is neither Kismet nor chaos. We narrow the range of possible futures by setting in motion sequential choices designed to make the future less problematic and more a reflection of national consensus. Such a consensus, which is at the root of all cooperative social action, is necessary if we are to ensure a comfortable and secure life for ourselves in the coming decades. Success in the short and long term depends, then, on the clarity of one's route and the commitment to shared goals. Knowing where you are going makes it easier to take in stride curves, detours, and adversities.

THE TRUE MEANING OF SURVIVAL AND PROSPERITY

To define a widely shared goal, it is essential to start with a fundamental or even universal value. No value could be more universal and no path more desirable than that leading to survival. Like many words, however, the core meaning of survival has become blurred and dulled by common usage. The word, derived from the Latin "supervivere"—to live over or beyond—translated literally means "super-life." Setting a goal of survival does not mean a society simply will live on, as a dynasty might weather crises such as plagues, droughts, or wars. A society survives—in fact, realizes its full potential—when its members share the goal of fulfilling needs for food, shelter, and clothing and bettering themselves with education, safety, health, liberty, and the chance to wonder at truth, beauty, and the divine.

The original definition of survival meshes perfectly with a national goal of prosperity, a word that also has become distorted over time. From the Latin "prosperitas," prosperity simply means success. Stripped of the connotations with which conspicuous consumption has tarnished it and combined with the goal of survival, prosperity is a national goal that would lead the United States to succeed in achieving the highest—most productive—future possible.

This book examines the ways to achieve prosperity and survival from several different perspectives. It offers a detailed scenario of economic and energy choices that can secure economic and energy well-being. It spells out specific policies that, if followed, will relieve the tensions between business and government and labor and management. And it presents—as inspiration—profiles of ten men and women who have encouraged survival and prosperity in their own lives by responding positively to change and accommodating chance.

The central question of this book is: How do we ensure the survival of our democratic society and its free enterprise system and simultaneously promote national prosperity? The combination of old perils (cycles of inflation and depression, uncertain supplies of food, water, and other resources, and war) and new threats (shortages of energy, an environment that has suffered at the hands of its inhabitants, and a failure of leadership to provide national direction) forms the sobering challenge of the future. If such perils and threats could be banished or wished away, Earth would have been a paradise long ago. But, by working in concert with each other and by making wise choices, citizens can ameliorate these conditions and create a better life.

2
Navigational Hazards

Having set forth a goal, we need to realistically assess the obstacles to achieving it. We can see at the outset that the course to prosperity is lined with many hazards challenging our navigational skills. The problems are well known: the economy, energy and other resources, the environment, the threat of nuclear annihilation, and the lack of effective leadership. Much has been written over the past decade about such difficulties, limits, and crises. For this reason a detailed review is not necessary here. An overview and some highlights are all that is needed.

THE ECONOMY AT LOW TIDE

Unemployment, slumping productivity, government deficits, high interest rates, stalled economic growth, and trade imbalances: to many U.S. citizens, these terms are like the colors and forms in an abstract painting; their effects are felt even though the ways in which they work are not really understood. In fact, many individuals comprehend economics only through personal experience: not being able to buy a house or to sustain one's standard of living or, worse, being out of work, makes painful economic lessons. In 1983 unemployment hovered around 10 percent. But firsthand exposure to double-digit inflation in the 1970s and huge federal deficits in the 1980s does not automatically produce a full understanding of the nation's complex financial life. To most individuals, the meanings of larger concepts, such as government deficits or productivity, still remain elusive, as do the numbers that quantify them. The U.S. federal debt, for example, is almost $1 trillion. A trillion dollars (a 1 with 12 zeroes) in 50 dollar bills could not be stuffed into all the pyramids in Egypt. The interest on this debt alone is $100 billion a year. Using $100 billion in $100 bills, a steeplejack could construct 72 stacks from the sidewalk reaching to the top of the tower on the Empire State Building, and on the seventy-third stack he would continue until the eighty-seventh floor. Think of the inner cities the United States could reclaim with this interest alone.

High debts and inflation were symptoms of the nation's declining economic health over the last decade. Until the late 1960s, growth rates in the United States were robust. Overall economic growth reached 4.1 percent per year, declining to an annual percentage of 2.9 in the 1970s. In 1981 the U.S. annual per capita income ranked tenth among Western industrialized countries. In 1960 U.S. industry supplied 95 percent of the domestic market for radios and televisions. In 1979 imports had claimed 50 percent of this market. Housing is a basic element in the standard of living. In 1981 the United States built 6.6 dwellings per 1,000 inhabitants compared to Japan's 14.7 and Greece's 14.2 percent per 1,000.

These numbers—indicators of change in our national standing—should be hard to take for U.S. citizens who dote on statistics that verify national achievement. When it comes to who is number one in the college ranks and who hit the most home runs in the big leagues, many people are well informed. They know that if a team wins 98 games, for example, it goes into the playoffs. But the numbers that explain our national economy inspire less interest—both as numbers and in terms of what is wrong with the team.

At the root is weak-hitting productivity. Productivity gauges how well and how expertly people work: it measures how much labor and investment people put in relative to what they turn out. Once the United States was the most productive team in its league. In the last few years, however, it has finished behind West Germany, Japan, and France.

Between 1960 and 1973, U.S. productivity grew at an annual rate of more than 3 percent: in other words, workers improved their performance every year that much. But since 1973, productivity growth dropped to 1.4 percent per year. From 1978 through 1980, labor productivity actually declined in absolute terms. There is a direct relationship between productivity and inflation. When productivity improves, it spreads each dollar of labor costs among a larger quantity of goods and in this way restrains price increases.

Productivity improvement depends heavily on private citizens' taking risks in the form of capital investment. In the 1970s, as factories and tools grew older and less efficient, leading foreign competitors set a brisk pace and then outdistanced the United States in investing in capital goods. Such investment—the key to increasing productivity—enabled foreign workers to work more efficiently. The United States kept up its economic output by a relatively fast growth in the labor force, but productivity per worker declined. The nation employed more labor instead of investing in more efficient but expensive new plant and equipment. The inevitable result of lower labor productivity was higher prices followed by a prolonged period of stagnation in a sea of economic doldrums.

Lying under the surface of the economic low tide is a basic shift in the structure of the economy and its engines of growth. In the 30 years following World War II, those engines were manufacturing (led by automobile sales), housing construction, and the interstate highway program started in 1956. More cars required more roads and highways, which made possible the growth of suburbs with housing farther from central cities. This in turn made a second car a necessity, and so on, and so on.

This interlocking relationship no longer works. The interstate highway system is virtually complete, housing starts peaked in 1972 with a high of 2.4 million units, and domestic automobile sales peaked the following year at 9.7 million cars. The question is whether high technology or something else can replace the combination of cars, highways, and housing as the engine of economic growth. The answer to this question is discussed at length in Chapter 4.

Economic productivity depends on an educated and skilled work force. The Education Commission of the United States has estimated that in 1990 about 2.5 million students will graduate from the nation's high schools and that about 80 percent of those will be unemployable because they will be technologically illiterate. Thus a failing education system is a major source of economic problems.

ENERGY: A SHIFTING CURRENT

For many years oil has been our most important single source of energy and, as such, has fueled much of our economy. It has helped determine how citizens live—from the proliferation of the suburbs to the convenience of throw-away items. But the world is depleting oil supplies. In the past decade, the general public has been made well aware of the certainty that oil companies have known and by which they have set policy for a long time. These companies knew they would have to discover as much oil every year as they pumped, or they would run out of inventory sooner or later, which is one of the reasons why U.S. and British companies went into the Middle East after World War I. The inevitability of depletion persuaded Congress to grant tax relief to companies that, by virtue of doing business, necessarily used up what they had to sell.

Oil production in the United States peaked in the 1970s. Even with new recovery techniques, reserves that do not exist cannot be used. At the present rates of consumption, or even if those rates gradually decline, supplies of oil will begin running short early in the next century. Conservation helps but it cannot increase the supply.

The Global 2000 Report to the President estimates that "During the 1990s world oil production will approach geological estimates of maximum capacity even with rapidly increasing petroleum prices. The Study projects that the richer industrialized nations will be able to command enough oil and other commercial energy supplies to meet rising demands through 1990."* Many developing countries will have much more difficulty meeting energy needs. One quarter of the world population still depends primarily on wood for fuel, and for them the outlook is bleak.

The Arab oil embargo of 1973 made painfully clear what an uncertain or emptying energy pump means to an economy. The rising cost of international oil fanned inflation. Tourist areas suffered a depressed summer because motorists stayed at home. Detroit had to begin hastily designing gas-efficient cars. The northeast United States,

---

*Council on Environmental Quality and the Department of State, *The Global 2000 Report to the President* (Washington, D.C.: Government Printing Office, 1980), p. 2.

with greater dependence on imported oil for home heating and fewer refineries than the rest of the nation, faced a fierce winter in 1973. The lesson was clear: the United States needed to stop postponing its transition from oil to other fuels.

Of course, U.S. citizens have weathered transitions before. Wood was once this nation's primary fuel. It powered the first locomotives and steamboats and heated the homes of colonists and pioneers. Then coal supplanted wood. It was cheaper and more plentiful. It could be mined and shipped in large quantities. Oil, in turn, supplanted coal because it was even cheaper and cleaner. These transitions from wood to coal to oil took place gradually over extended periods of time. Time to develop new fuel sources and convert from oil, however, is short.

Under this pressure the nation is shifting to a variety of alternative and renewable energy sources as well as maintaining its reliance on coal and nuclear fuel. Until the transition from oil to other fuels is complete, energy costs will remain high. In the case of oil, high means that prices will not return to the levels preceding the 1973 oil embargo. OPEC may have difficulty maintaining control of prices in the early 1980s, but after a period of adjustment demand will work to assure that oil will never again be a cheap source of energy.

In the past and in the present, U.S. citizens have mitigated the effects of high oil prices by consciously choosing to conserve all forms of energy. They conserve both out of patriotic impulses and because of economic necessity. Many have lowered their thermostats and added insulation to their homes. Others use mass transit or have joined car pools.

Because energy touches almost everyone directly, it has received a great deal of attention in the past ten years. But it is not the only resource vital to our national well-being. The United States imports tin, manganese, cadmium, and other strategic metals also not in infinite supply. These resources are potentially subject to the same problems we face with energy.

OTHER RESOURCES: SOIL AND WATER

The most basic resources are food-producing soil and life-giving water. The world may house over 6 billion people in 2000, an increase of more than 50 percent since 1975. It still can produce enough food for its population, but it will have to make extreme demands on its crop lands, which steadily shrink as nature itself takes a toll. The Mississippi River, for example, washes away 250 million tons of crop lands every year. Land is also lost to industrial and urban use. Farmland becomes highways, airports, shopping centers, industrial parks, military bases, subdivision housing developments, and reservoirs at a rate of 12 square miles a day. Ultimately, this means higher food prices.

Despite U.S. food surpluses and exports, people the world over suffer from food shortages. Food is the Soviet Union's most serious problem. In 1981 the late President Leonid Brezhnev reported the grain harvest would dip below 175 million tons, more than 60 million tons under the official quota, amounting to the worst crop in six years. The perennial Soviet food shortages are compounded by distribution problems which, in fact, have become a global problem. While the world produces enough food to feed its people, transportation systems often do not exist to move surpluses to areas of scarcity. Crops rot on the ground, and 10 percent is lost to rodents and insects because of insecure storage facilities. More people, less farmland, and faulty distribution means increasing hunger and actual starvation. World need will tax U.S. resources, for this country is the largest food producer.

Water, another life-giving resource, is necessary for growing food, and water supplies throughout the world are being depleted. In the United States, ground water levels are being pumped down all over the country. The Ogalala Aquifer, which extends from the Dakotas to Texas, has dropped at an alarming rate. Pollution continues to threaten usable water supplies, despite increased investment in water treatment equipment. The problem is not confined to the United States; it is global. The Soviet Union's Aral Sea, the fourth largest inland body on earth, is drying up because Soviet engineers diverted its waters to irrigate central Asia. At the present rate of decline, 18 inches a year, the Aral Sea, which covers 25,500 square miles, will disappear in 20 years.

Similar conditions afflict the Orient. In Peking the population of 8.5 million people has been depleting underground water supplies for 15 years. In recent years the rate of usage has been nearly twice the rate of replacement. The water level under Peking fell more than 4 feet in the past year and more than 25 feet in the last three decades, leaving a 400-square-mile hollow under the city.

ENVIRONMENTAL CHALLENGES

The most chilling lesson of the past few decades appears to be that all of humanity's activities—industrial and social—have had some deleterious effects on the environment, which supplies the raw materials and energy to fuel social progress. Excessive demands on the ecological system can cause a spiraling downturn in the resource base and productivity. This is observable all over the world— in Africa where the Sahara desert is expanding, in islands such as Haiti and the Malagasy Republic, and in the United States as well. The heavily irrigated San Joaquin Valley in California has a growing problem of salinization. This is an age-old agricultural problem, which contributed to the decline of the ancient region of Sumer, whose soil, ruined by thousands of years of irrigation, has never recovered. Inexorable laws of cause and effect govern the environment and the pollution of it. Today, scientists understand much more about the nature of pollution effects and what can be done to migitate them. But this is a costly process. In addition to money it requires time and an easing of pressures on the land.

Prosperity allows a significant percentage of the nation's income to be directed toward the preservation of the environment, and thoughtful analysis can direct that income where benefits will best be realized. Without a sufficient level of prosperity, this necessary money will not exist, and the environment inevitably will go begging. The saying, "There are few environmentalists in the ghetto," applies not only to the United States but to the developing world as well.

More than ever, signs clearly point to the essential role that environmental research plays in securing our safety and that of future generations. As the effects of pollution have been discovered, corrective measures have been devised to minimize their toll. Currently, much attention has been focused on two environmental phenomena—acid rain and the so-called greenhouse effect—and considerable money and talent is being directed at determining scientifically how humanity's industrial activity contributes to or exacerbates these conditions. Although there is no conclusive evidence that either of these conditions is exclusively man-made or that they present proven dangers to our population, an informal coalition of industry, government, and the scientific community is addressing these issues systematically. As modern men and women have become more aware of the environmental side effects of their activities—such as pollution and resource depletion—they are determined to confront these problems before it is too late.

Consequently, citizens have a vested interest in better long-term strategies and decision making. Take, for example, a social need for more housing. The builder who puts up a new development may serve this social need, but one cost of the new construction may be the loss of plant and wildlife habitat. This process is magnified many times over in the rain forests of Third World countries. The plant and animal life in tropical zones is extremely diverse. Deforestation threatens the permanent loss of thousands of species. In developing countries 40 percent of the remaining forest cover could be gone by the year 2000.

Every day marks the extinction of another plant or animal. The world's genetic pool, the stock of nature's raw materials, is shrinking. This pool supplies the very elements of future food supplies, chemicals, medicines, and other compounds. About half of the drugs on the market today were derived from living organisms. The field of genetic engineering is just in its infancy. It is important to preserve the gene pool so that genes can be recombined. Genes are very complicated and if they are lost, they cannot be replaced. We are collectively throwing away elements that future generations of people can use to improve their own conditions. The rate at which species are being lost is increasing. By 1990 it may accelerate to one species an hour, a situation with distinct national security implications. Even now the United States is heavily dependent on foreign supplies of genetic material. Without germ plasm to help create a variety of hybrid fruits and vegetables, the public would have a limited diet. We rely on seeds and cuttings imported by agricultural specialists to create food variety. As this country learned irrefutably during the 1973 oil embargo, resource dependency of any kind is a serious disadvantage.

Thus the costs of environmental negligence can be more far-reaching than we first realized. Too often humanity has exploited the environment purely for convenience or profit. We have polluted rivers with waste, poisoned the air with smoke and noxious fumes, and desecrated the woodlands. We are now paying the price: the environment, once polluted, poisoned, and desecrated, threatens health, prosperity, and life itself.

ENTROPY: THE THREAT OF WINDING DOWN

Some economic theorists subsume the formidable problems of energy, earth, food, water, and environmental pollution under the law of entropy. This fundamental principle, the second law of thermodynamics, holds that the universe tends toward randomness rather than organization. It is running down like a wristwatch that cannot be rewound. Energy is transformed into heat, which inevitably passes from hot to cold, never the reverse. As energy is used, it is dissipated, never to be recaptured. The same law applies to matter. Entropy is matter and energy reduced to its lowest state with its least potential for work, like ashes in a fire. Any use of energy and material increases total entropy.

Economic growth, some writers have argued, only increases entropy by creating more waste heat and refuse, despite society's recycling efforts. Energy winds up as carbon dioxide, machines eventually wear out, and books disintegrate on library shelves. These theorists would control economic activity, imposing strict limits on growth, since, in their view, nature cannot replenish itself. Moreover, by the process of extrapolation, such analysts claim these physical laws of thermodynamics as the authority for their prophecies of heightening scarcity and economic decline.

Ironically, it is in the testing of this profoundly pessimistic view that the basis for hope about the future emerges. According to the law of entropy, society should be growing less organized, less complex, and less diverse; yet, when we look around us, the opposite seems true. In fact, life and society grow more complex and present a greater diversity of choices with each passing day and decade. Moreover, while matter follows physical laws, societies and economies apparently do not. Composed of individuals imbued with the sparks of intelligence and creativity, societies resist entropic movement as men and women exert a powerful force of their own toward order and against entropy. And the natural decay that does occur is at rates that hardly warrant the concern that alarmists would have us feel. The Egyptian pyramid builders thought their work would last forever. And while the pyramids are subject to erosion, the process is, in the final analysis, imperceptible. The pyramids, like all of humanity's accomplishments, inspire us to believe that intelligence and creativity can counter the effects of entropy. When we examine the byproducts of our collective intelligence more closely, they offer striking evidence for our durability. As a living social system, we have developed methods of transmitting the fruits of our intelligence from one generation to another via education. Another quality that has contributed to staving off the threat of entropy is humanity's capacity to change—what scientists call mutability. We have proven ourselves to be quite adroit at adapting to a changing environment. In another vein, the way in which our society uses energy and gives off waste imitates the way that all life forms exchange energy with the environment. Indeed, achieving organization and intelligence demands energy. It is only through the infusion of energy that order can be maintained. Since almost all energy on earth ultimately comes from the sun, it is good to know that the sun has enough energy to burn for another 5 to 8 billion years. Lastly, just as higher forms of life are capable of free movement, our society has developed its capacities for mobility, thereby continually expanding horizons that were once finite. The process of learning through interaction with the environment is described very well by Viola Spolin, a producer, director, and writer. "We learn through experience and experiencing and no one teaches anyone anything. This is as true for the infant moving from kicking to crawling to walking as it is for the scientist with his equations. If the environment permits it, anyone can learn whatever he chooses to learn; and if the individual permits it, the environment will teach him everything it has to teach."*

The way in which people exercise their intelligence and creativity will determine the degree of prosperity our society will enjoy as well as our potential to survive future threats. In fact, there is less danger that we will wear ourselves out than that we will blow ourselves up.

NUCLEAR WAR: THE ULTIMATE HAZARD

Enough nuclear armaments exist today to kill every man, woman, and child in the world 12 times over. Spending for destructive purposes among all nations exceeds $1 billion a day, and the present

---

*Viola Spolin, *Improvisation for the Threatre* (Evanston, Ill.: Northwestern University Press, 1963), p. 3.

worldwide stock of nuclear warheads equals an explosive power of 1 million Hiroshima-sized atomic bombs. If all of these weapons were released, the damage would defy all imagination; it is unlikely that life on Earth would survive the effects.

The population of the United States is unprepared for nuclear war because preparation is impossible. Those not killed in the initial blasts would suffer from radiation sickness and grievous injuries and would find no help. There would be no facilities to provide treatment for survivors suffering radiation sickness. Care for such casualties includes bed rest, nursing and other supportive services. The government's stockpiling of 130,000 pounds of opium to meet "essential civilian needs" reveals the hopelessness of the situation. There would in fact be no means of distribution and administration of that opium.

While strategists consider nuclear arms deterrents to a first strike, these weapons do not, in fact, confer security. Like any weapon, they can be released by mere miscalculation. In 1979 the computers of the North American Air Defense Command warned the Pentagon of a Soviet-launched nuclear attack; a computer tape simulating attack by submarine-launched missiles had mistakenly been plugged in. We depend upon the reliability of both electronic components as small as a dime and humans subject to fatigue, boredom, and judgmental errors under stress to determine the fate of the world.

These are awesome considerations. But that has not stopped the United States from making plans to add $1.6 trillion in military spending through 1986 to "rearm" the nation. Under this plan, defense outlays would rise from a current 24 percent of the federal budget to 31 percent in 1984 and 38 percent in 1986. In a time of economic crisis brought about by federal budget deficits, it is questionable whether increased defense spending adds to overall national security.

In addition to the physical threat it poses, the arms race is a monumental economic drain for its participants. People have to pay for arms with either higher taxes, which slows economic growth, or a higher national debt, which fuels the fires of inflation. Trying to improve on the ultimate weapon and matching the other side bomb for bomb, regardless of the rate of escalation, means lowering the standard of living and allocating fewer goods and services for citizens.

But the arms race exacts an even greater price than economic sacrifices. Far from providing security in the individual's mind, nuclear weapons and the arms race induce anxiety and moral paralysis. Choices based on fear do not lead to survival, much less to prosperity. Continuation of the arms race can have only two outcomes: total annihilation or economic exhaustion.

Unilateral disarmament is clearly not a viable path to survival, either. So the only fruitful course will be negotiation of mutual arms reductions.

WHO IS AT THE WHEEL?

As old perils and new threats combine to block our pathways to prosperity, the need for leadership and consensus decision making becomes more acute. But lacking a sense of shared purpose, citizens cannot expect even the best leadership to solve national problems alone. A variety of conflicting interests—consumer and environmental concerns, union rules, and government regulations—make the arena in which elected officials operate a turbulent one of contradictory claims and pressing interests.

The threats of public disdain, media sensationalism, and constituent apathy (to name but three) render public life both less glamorous and less rewarding than it might seem. Thus the constraints on leaders and on consensus building are themselves threats to survival and prosperity. Leadership has become a process of negotiating, pleading, satisfying, avoiding, protecting, and getting by. As a result of these pressures, many leaders quit in frustration. For example, Ohio's Thirteenth Congressional District representative, Charles A. Mosher, wrote to his constituents in 1976:

> Being the Congressman is rigorous servitude, ceaseless enslavement to a particular mix of everyone else's needs, demands and whims, plus one's sense of duty, ambition or vanity. It is that from which Mrs. Mosher and I now declare our personal independence, to seek our freedom, as of January 3, 1977.
>
> It is a Congressman's inescapable lot, his or her enslavement, to be never alone, never free from incessant buffeting by people, events, problems, decisions. . . . It is a grueling experience, often frustrating, discouraging, sometimes very disillusioning . . . house debates, caucuses, briefings, working breakfasts, working lunches, receptions, dinners, homework study, and even midnight collect calls from drunks . . . you name it. I am for opting out.

Congressman Mosher is not alone. According to a report in the *Legislative Studies Quarterly*, 153 representatives voluntarily renounced public life between 1972 and 1980. This compares with 81 members who left between 1962 and 1970.*

Ultimately, the public determines the success of its leaders. The public must be willing to commit itself to a course and to see it through so that the results of the chosen policies can be fairly judged. In a free society, rights imply associated duties. Chief among these is supporting the good of the whole. Lacking political consensus, we have government by coalition of special interest groups, an inherently unstable and confusing process. Under such circumstances an exasperated majority has more than once given over its freedoms to a strong and charismatic person who promised stability. Our future depends on choosing strong leaders able to rally public consensus and commitment and then supporting the chosen direction over the long pull. Any captain needs a disciplined crew.

The hazards and problems are formidable. It is, after all, easier to describe bad effects of bad causes than to identify good causes leading to good results. But however imposing the challenges facing us in the 1980s, they are no greater than those our predecessors weathered. We possess the intelligence and the resources to convert obstacles into opportunities; doing so is a matter of making choices, of the willingness to take risks, and of the ability to change.

Humanity's history is the history of choices, risks, and change, and every generation before us has met its demands, which is why we are here today. Choices are available to us that offer a path to a prosperous and secure future; we must recognize and act on those choices and thereby preserve the right of self-determination.

---

*John R. Hibbing, "Voluntary Retirement From the U.S. House: The Costs of Congressional Service," *Legislative Studies Quarterly* (February 1982).

3
A Preferred Path

A journey requires an itinerary, a plan leading to a specific destination. A map shows many ways to get from point A to point B, but usually one route is better than others—a preferred path. In narrative form, such a map becomes a scenario with a beginning, middle, and end along with a basic plot holding things all together. Such a map is needed to highlight anticipated landmarks and events.

BUILDING A SCENARIO

Any number of different kinds of scenarios exist, ranging from the plot synopses of the silent movies to the products of computerized economic forecasting models. Economists who construct scenarios start with judgments and assumptions. Given the assumptions, they can say what the likely outcome would be. The surgeon general of the United States, for example, could write a scenario promoting longevity that would include scenes of prenatal care, periodic examinations, dental hygiene, and a healthy diet. But his scenario would in no way guarantee every person who followed the plan a long and vigorous life. People die in auto accidents, commit suicide, develop fatal diseases—events or contingencies not subject to prediction or control. The scenario simply proposes a goal and recommends the means by which most people who want to live a long life can achieve their goal.

Another example of a scenario might posit parents who want their child to attend Yale and who, as a consequence, will have to start preparing the child academically and also start saving for the tuition. This decision by no means guarantees their offspring's admission to Yale. Some teenagers drop out of high school; some do not meet entrance requirements; some marry early; some choose other schools. But if the child's parents or the child do not make adequate provisions early, there will be no chance when the time comes for admission.

Many people incorrectly assume that modeling potential economic futures is strictly a numerical enterprise. But, in an economic scenario, events are subjected to both quantitative and qualitative analyses. An economist may want to assume, for example, what the birth rate in the United States will be over the next two decades in order to determine the size of the work force to be employed in 2000. Thinking about the values and styles of living that will lead to that birth rate is a matter of qualitative judgment.

In addition to setting goals, a scenario can clarify cause-and-effect relationships. It is a way to get answers to "What if . . ." questions. If the work force absorbs a stable number of immigrants over the next 20 years, it suggests a certain level of housing demand. But if immigration decreases, one expects a need for less housing, a need that ripples across the economy in terms of other goods.

This book proposes a "preferred" scenario, a description of the personal and public policy choices that would lead to survival and prosperity over a 20-year period. The preferred scenario pictures positive actions leading through the hazards described in Chapter 2, despite adverse chance factors. Other scenarios are possible, including doomsday forecasts and utopian designs. This preferred scenario is drawn from a detailed analysis reported in *Choice over Chance: Economic and Energy Options for the Future.*[*] The preferred scenario, among the several developed, is not only desirable

---

[*]William F. Thompson, Jerome J. Karaganis, and Kenneth D. Wilson, *Choice over Chance: Economic and Energy Options for the Future* (New York: Praeger, 1981).

but within reach. It does not rely on good luck emanating from factors outside our control; in fact, it assumes bad luck.

How is such a scenario constructed? First, a set of assumptions about starting points is made and then fed into an economic model. A computer-based economic model is a collection of mathematical formulas that simulate quantitatively the interaction of factors within a system—a system such as the U.S. economy. The formulas come from empirically verified statistics. For example, the Bureau of the Census can count the workers within the economy; economists have fashioned elaborate indexes to measure various aspects of economic performance and have formulated and verified relationships, for example, among the birth and immigration rates and economic output. Modelers employ a host of factors such as these to create one element of an economic model. A particularly crucial formula examines the relationship between productivity and capital investment: as capital investment declines, productivity stagnates and then declines.

A complex and dynamic economy is made up of thousands of such relationships. The equations and models that replicate them are evolved by teams of economists who spend years refining these interrelated equations and testing them to see if they hold up over time. It is an art and science called econometrics. Refined models, such as the five on which *Choice over Chance* was based, fill many volumes.

Only the capability of computers makes it possible to handle the calculations necessary for sophisticated modeling exercises. When economists feed in assumed policy choices such as federal tax rates, energy regulations, and rates of saving or spending, the machine prints out an econometric scenario—how the economy could be expected to perform over time.

While many models deal with discrete aspects of the economy, only a few comprehensive ones exist. The models most treasured as state of the art, and those upon which this book's analysis is based, are forecasting jewels. The Hudson-Jorgenson model, which projects energy and economic growth patterns, served as the foundation for this analysis. The Wharton annual model, which deals with demand economics, and the Evans Economic Inc. model, which focuses on the supply side, further expanded the modeling exercises to refine the potential scenarios. The ETA-Macro model was employed to examine long-term energy and economic futures. The Baughman-

Joskow model supplemented the patterns analyzed by the Hudson-Jorgenson model.

Choice over Chance examined two primary scenarios besides the preferred path. A high-growth scenario foresaw a prosperous future brought about by uninterrupted good luck. "Good luck" denoted a slow rise in oil prices unmarred by emergencies and a fast rate of technological advances. Policy choices led to tax reform, which increased savings and investment. Individual choices led to a higher birth rate and an expanding labor force. A low-growth scenario anticipated decreasing birth rates and, therefore, a smaller and less skilled labor force, with workers working fewer hours each week. In this scenario, rising corporate and personal income taxes inhibit investment, and bad luck takes the form of escalating oil prices. The preferred scenario, the third principal future, presumes bad luck on matters out of policy control but relies on the reasonable implementation of wise choices.

The preferred path was reached by specifying a desired future state in terms of a few basic variables and working backwards to pinpoint the multiple choices that have to be made now and until the year 2000 to bring about that result. Those with experience know that chance will interrupt any sequence of choices, no matter how wise. Therefore, assumptions about economically important chance factors were incorporated into the modeling exercise to make the results as realistic as possible.

The world price of oil, for example, is a crucial chance factor. Chance can be advantageous; that is, world oil prices can drop. Or it can be disadvantageous; world oil prices can rise. One thing is certain about the effect of chance on our lives: when striving for survival—indeed for prosperity—sensible individuals will not count on good luck but, instead, will prepare for the worst. If the worst fails to happen, so much the better.

Among the modeling assumptions employed for this analysis, 13 economic factors depend primarily upon choices that are indeed ours to make, factors over which we can and historically have exercised much control. Five factors place us exclusively at the mercy of chance. The total 18 factors are divided into five groups, which include all of the assumptions fed into the computer models to achieve the preferred scenario.

The first group, *demographic* factors, consists of (1) the fertility rate of women and (2) immigration rates. *Labor force* factors, the second group, consist of the participation by (3) males and (4) females in the work force and the hours worked each week by (5) men and (6) women. The third group, *productivity* factors, includes (7) the average annual rate of growth in gross labor productivity, (8) the percentage of GNP devoted to private investment, (9) the percentage devoted to government investment, and (10) the average annual rate of investment in environmental protection. *Fiscal policy* factors consist of (11) the personal income tax rate, (12) the corporate income tax rate, and (13) the investment tax credit rate. The fifth group, and the one in which chance most affects us, is *world energy*, represented by (14) the world price of oil, which has recently dominated and will probably continue to dominate the other factors: (15) the price of coal, (16) the amount of solar energy produced, (17) the amount of synthetic energy produced, and (18) the amount of nuclear energy produced.

Of course, other chance events could significantly affect our lives: climate changes, loss of biological diversity, and nuclear war are three. The first two will have important effects in the longer-term future, while the third cannot readily be modeled. Energy was chosen as the major chance variable because of its crucial near-term consequences.

The preferred scenario is presented in two forms: first, in overall economic outline with aggregate national policies and numbers; second, as a narrative of the lives and personal choices of three fictional U.S. citizens. The human and personal context is a way of making the large numbers in the national scenario alive and familiar. Stories are easier to relate to than figures.

The national overview is made up of the input assumptions and the outputs from the econometric models. Its cornerstone is the gross national product.

GNP—THE FOUNDATION

The gross national product, also known as the GNP, is not a perfect measurement of an economy's performance, but it is the most widely accepted. It is as if the GNP is a pie whose overall size in turn determines how big a slice individual citizens can expect. The preferred scenario found it feasible to set an economic goal of a 3 percent rise in the gross national product each year for the next

20 years. Compounded annually, this growth in real GNP will quadruple the income of the poorest 20 percent of the nation's families, double the income of the next 20 percent, and make positive improvements in the income of the remaining 60 percent. In short, if the pie gets bigger, more people can move up to the table and get a bigger piece.

The benefits of economic growth for the poor are not a matter of theory or hope. According to an analysis by Charles Murray, former chief scientist of the American Institutes for Research, the economic growth of the 1950s was much more effective in reducing poverty than the "War on Poverty" programs of the 1960s. Due mostly to economic growth, the number of people living below the poverty level declined from 33 percent of the population in 1949 to 18 percent in 1964. The number dropped to 13 percent by 1968. During the next five years, when the poverty programs were in high gear, progress actually slowed. The percentage of people living in poverty declined to 11 percent in 1973 but returned to 13 percent in 1980. Murray believes that the social welfare policies increased dependency and encouraged family breakups. He concludes that economic growth is the only real cure for poverty.*

In 1978 per capita income after taxes actually was $6,300 in 1978 dollars. In the high-growth scenario, real after-tax income at the end of the century would amount to $11,400 per person, a projected 80 percent increase. In the low-growth scenario, real income would amount to only $8,061. The real per capita income projection in the preferred scenario rises to $10,228. That amounts to over $30,000 in today's dollars for an average family of three. Thus prosperity equals $30,000 per year.

Calling for a 3 percent rise in our GNP is hardly whistling in the dark. In the recent past GNP has grown for short times at rates as fast as 6 or 7 percent. From 1960 to 1969 it grew at the rate of 4.3 percent. It did not grow at all in 1981 and decreased 1.8 percent in 1982, a fact that reflects not only widespread unemployment but deepening poverty, both of which have historically portended change in governments and economies.

---

*Charles A. Murray, "The Two Wars Against Poverty: Economic Growth and the Great Society," *The Public Interest*, Fall 1982.

POPULATION TRENDS

For the preferred scenario, the analysis assumed a fertility rate of 2.1 children per women—bare replacement for the population.

Between 1958 and 1963, the birth rate was 3.5. This period was a prosperous one for the country, and prosperity usually means increased family size. The low birth rate of the Great Depression years meant less competition for jobs in the 1950s and 1960s. Workers improved their economic condition faster, married earlier, and had less need for a second income. Consequently, people raised larger families. Children of a high birth-rate cycle meet more competition for jobs and earn appreciably less than senior members of the labor force. Consequently, they defer marriage and families.

The birth rate began to drop in the mid-1960s for economic reasons, not to mention the popularity and easy availability of new contraceptive techniques. A third cause limiting the size of the family has been a growing concern about world overpopulation—to some, a moral factor. Another intangible is the desire and pursuit of leisure. Thus, at the beginning of the 1980s, the birth rate in the United States was 1.8. Birth rates are a matter of personal choice, and the preferred scenario assumes that we will choose to replace ourselves.

Death rates declined from 9.9 deaths per year per 1,000 in 1948 to 9.5 in 1970. Life expectancy has risen from 68.2 years in 1950 to 73.2 in 1977. According to biologists and experts in the field of geriatrics, medical breakthroughs probably will lengthen life expectancy dramatically and therefore prolong working life. Counting on some modest prolongation, the preferred scenario makes a realistic assumption and aligns it with reasonable trends.

THE IMPACT OF IMMIGRATION

Immigrants are important to a nation's economy because they join the work force immediately. For the past decade, the immigration of foreigners into the United States officially has numbered 400,000 yearly. But this is an official fiction. Illegal immigration from Mexico alone probably totals 500,000 a year, although many of these people do not take up permanent residence here. There is continuing strong pressure from Mexico, the Caribbean countries,

Latin America, and the Far East for more liberal immigration laws in the United States, but the laws are irrelevant. There is no practical way to control the U.S.-Mexican border. As in the case of Prohibition, a law that cannot be enforced is really not a law.

Thus the preferred scenario anticipates that every year an additional 300,000 immigrants will join this country's population over and above the 400,000 predicted by the Bureau of Immigration.

WORK DEFINES THE COMMUNITY

At the end of the 1970s, 103 million men and women composed the labor force. From 1950 to 1978, the fraction of all females 16 years of age and older in the labor force rose from one-third to one-half. Over the same period, male participation rates dropped from 88 to 78 percent. Some analysts attribute these recent shifts to changing styles of living; others to better living standards. The change in the female participation rate has been the most dramatic, and there is much controversy about why women have entered the labor force in increasing numbers. Have they gone to work in order to raise family living standards? Or have more women decided that the rewards of motherhood and homemaking are less desirable than the rewards of careers? Or, as increasing numbers have proven, are these pursuits not mutually exclusive?

The preferred scenario assumes the continuation of current trends toward an equalization of the numbers of working men and working women. The number of men working will shift from 78 percent at present to 75 percent in the year 2000. The number of women will increase from the current 49 percent to 60 percent.

The manufacturing workweek decreased from 60 hours in 1890 to 40 hours a half century later. Since then, it has remained relatively stable. But the workweek in other industries continues to grow shorter—from 1950 to 1979, the insurance and real estate professions declined to 36 hours and government to 35.

The contemporary U.S. citizen is working about as long a workweek as did serfs in the Middle Ages. The serf was bound over to the feudal baron or apprenticed to the master for as many hours a week as either chose to work him. But in the Middle Ages, every other day was a religious holiday or a saint's day, which spared the apprentice or the serf a great many hours a week of grueling toil.

The preferred scenario estimates that the workweek of the labor force will decline to 33 hours per week for men and 31 hours per week for women by the year 2000. Over the years, no factors in our economy have changed as radically as those associated with work—not only the components of the labor force but the attitudes about work that characterize them—attitudes that are evolving continuously.

The Protestant work ethic emerged as a strong societal force during the Industrial Revolution. This ethic insists that work not only rewards but ennobles. The ethic often was perverted, however, because ever more ennoblement was thrust upon workers in lieu of rewards. In the course of this revolution, work seemed to lose its aesthetic component and came to be seen as something demeaning. Nevertheless, a secularized Protestant work ethic remains a familiar, if perhaps less commanding, imperative as we enter the 1980s.

Work is one of the main ways individuals define themselves and make contributions to the community. Work also provides a means to realize one's self-worth in a manner independent of other external rewards: the love of a spouse, the respect of one's children, or the satisfaction of religious affirmation.

Because the structure of work really defines the community, as work changes, so does the society. From an agrarian society in the nineteenth century, with the bulk of its population living on farms, the United States became an industrial society in the first half of the twentieth century, with a population residing principally in cities. This complexion, too, has changed. In 1930, according to the United States Bureau of the Census, 28 percent of factory workers were unskilled blue-collar workers. In 1970 only 11 percent of factory workers were unskilled. Today, less than 15 percent of U.S. citizens work in factories as skilled or unskilled workers. The United States is no longer a basically industrial society. It has become an information/service society.

Measured against other work forces in the Western world, the U.S. work force has assimilated the highest infusion of new and inexperienced workers. Between 1948 and 1973, the work force expanded at a rate of 1.5 percent every year. Between 1973 and 1979, the work force expanded by 2.7 percent each year. Many of the new workers were untrained women of all ages, minorities, and the children of the postwar baby boom. The amount of investment per worker has declined accordingly; finding enough work for all has become more important than discovering who works efficiently at what.

Work in America, a landmark study of changing work patterns, documents the ways in which attitudes toward work have changed as work and the composition of the labor force have changed. Workers want to influence the mode of production; they want to feel a social value in their work (as, say, those who manufacture precision tools might feel better about their work than do those who manufacture pesticides); workers have expectations and they often believe that what they expect is different from what employers want to give; furthermore, workers want relief from the tedium of their jobs, and workers want employment as a natural right. They want communication with their fellow workers and with their superiors, and they want to believe that the employer is their partner, not someone who measures the performance of one employee against another.*

One approach to dealing with worker dissatisfaction has been a move to "humanize" work, to make it more varied, more interesting, and to develop more skills in the worker. This humanization of work may entail redesigning the work day and rearranging the tasks performed. Industries have been experimenting with the "working module," a time span of from two to four hours in which the worker performs one task before moving to another related task.

More complex—and so far more successful—is the concept of work teams to lighten the lot of assembly line workers. In the auto industry, management has organized the workers into teams of nine whose task is to assemble the entire car. Use of these teams has reduced defects and imperfections in the finished autos. Pragmatic economists and social scientists ask: "Does job satisfaction lead to increased productivity?" If the answer were an unqualified "yes," certain strategies for increasing productivity would be apparent. But in ordinary industrial situations no clear answer exists. Sometimes job satisfaction spurs production, while at other times the meanest tasks boost productive workers.

The length of our working life is changing, too. Presently, the common retirement age is 65, not only for Social Security recipients,

---

*Report of a Special Task Force to the Secretary of Health, Education and Welfare, *Work in America* (Cambridge, Mass.: MIT Press, 1972).

but for private and other public pension plans. These plans date from the 1920s and 1930s when few people lived longer than 65 years. Mandatory retirement at a certain age now has been ruled illegal by the courts. People in the 1980s and 1990s will enjoy much better, healthier, older years than their parents and grandparents, and a larger preponderance of them will live appreciably past 65. Most of these people also will want to continue working because they will find retirement income inadequate. Of course, this generation's education is often more sophisticated and fits them for jobs that make fewer physical demands. The need for productive workers at every level makes suspect the mandatory retirement of any healthy worker. Moreover, aging is a costly process, and some of these costs can be absorbed by lengthening the traditional span of a working life.

The population aged 65 years and older increases by 2 million individuals every five years. By 1985 there will be 27 million people who depend to some degree on Social Security, which will demand 26 percent of the federal budget for their support. By the turn of the century, 32 million people over 65 will need more than 30 percent of the federal budget. Accordingly, younger workers will have to pay a proportionately higher amount of taxes to support them. The practical way to meet this tax increase is to ask older workers to stay at their jobs longer. In the present work force, there are five people of working age for every person over 65. But when these five workers reach 65, for every one of them there will be only three and one-half younger persons working.

The working population of the country is shrinking in its relative size. For every three workers who can support a retired beneficiary today, two workers will have to support a beneficiary by the turn of the century. Each year 400,000 new claimants receive Social Security checks.

PRODUCTIVITY FOR ROBINSON CRUSOE—
FOR YOU AND ME

Possibly the most crucial single factor in the preferred scenario is productivity. It is the key to maintaining economic growth, reducing inflation, creating new jobs, competing in international trade, and enhancing the environment and the overall quality of life. What is productivity? It can be explained by the simple example of the island microeconomy of Robinson Crusoe and his man Friday. Picture an island and Crusoe and Friday working together over a number of years. In time the two men double their output even though they work the same number of hours per week. There is nothing mysterious about this; it is the result of improved productivity based on three factors. First, Crusoe and Friday constantly add to their stock of tools. From driftwood they build a rowboat, thereby *increasing capital goods.* Second, the two constantly improve upon their tools. Instead of rowing to their fishing grounds, they add a sail, which enables them to catch more fish in a shorter time, thus *increasing the efficiency of capital.* Both of these activities are forms of investment. Third, the two learn new skills and grow smarter about island survival. They read the winds and tides and chart the best fishing areas, which represents an *increase in the proficiency of labor.* An increase in the hours worked by Crusoe and Friday and/or the arrival of more stranded sailors would boost total worker hours and increase output, expanding gross island product or economic growth.

In our own economy, productivity improvement derives from the same three factors. Computer models represent these factors in terms of private investment, government investment, investment in environmental protection, and gross labor productivity.

For almost a century, the United States achieved an annual rate of 1.7 percent for total productivity and 2.4 percent in labor productivity. This meant that every 30 years U.S. productivity doubled. For the past 7 years, however, productivity has been growing at 0.23 percent. We need to boost this to 2.24 percent per year to achieve the preferred results.

To begin with, we must understand why our productivity growth rate has fallen. The following two illustrations should prove helpful. The Department of Sanitation of New York City ordered 220 new garbage trucks at a cost of $71,000 each. The goal was to improve productivity by using fewer men to collect more garbage. These sanitation trucks, which were loaded from the side instead of the rear, needed only two workers instead of three. Thus the new fleet freed at least 220 men for other equally important tasks, from street cleaning to painting playgrounds. The Uniformed Sanitationmen's Association won a share of these savings in salary raises for its members. But once in operation, the trucks' hydraulic systems developed difficulties. As a consequence, each truck hauled only 7.5 tons of garbage instead of its stated capacity of 9 tons. Many manhours were lost while the trucks were repaired by the manufacturer which, in turn, cut into his profits and operating costs. Sometimes garbage festered in the streets. And the Uniformed Sanitationmen's Association did not give back the raises.

A second illustration reveals the hidden costs that seriously inflate our defense budget. Contractors who win bids to produce military hardware ensure their firms years of work and millions of dollars in revenue. It is not surprising, therefore, that many contractors submit artificially low bids. Inevitably, there are overruns at which point specialists begin litigation, putting forward claims that cannot be adjudicated quickly, claims often as obscure as they are voluminous. In many cases, the military experts have authorized design changes that raise the price of a system but rarely to the astronomical sums for which the Pentagon settles.

The effect of this industrial-legal complex is most evident in navy contracting, because ships take much longer to build and are far more costly than other armaments. In 1978, for example, the government paid more than $1.1 billion in overruns for ships with three major contractors, even though navy analysts agreed that less than half that cost was justified. The navy paid the rest, fearing the cost of never-ending litigation over $2.7 billion in claims that eight law firms submitted for these contracts.

Productivity can be restored by increased investment in new and efficient capital goods. Many U.S. factories, tools, and processes are now outmoded, which is one of the reasons that other economies devastated by World War II that subsequently rebuilt have spurted ahead at rates two and three times greater than ours. Those economies restored their industrial bases on new technologies that increased production and its efficiency. Some of these economies, particularly West Germany and Japan, also were relieved of the expense of armaments.

Recent productivity increases in the United States are among the lowest of the industrial countries. Nor does the nose-diving purchasing power of the dollar help the problem. The productivity decline has halted growth in the buying power of U.S. workers. A study by the New York Stock Exchange found that the buying power of wages before taxes, but after adjusting for inflation, remained unchanged for the 12 years between 1967 and 1979. Between 1947 and 1965, 85 percent of the increased output in the private sector was derived from productivity improvements due to new plants, new products, and new technologies, and 15 percent were derived from increased labor input from more workers and fewer stoppages. By 1980, after years of lagging investment, the statistic had reversed, proving that productivity demands investment. If it is to survive and prosper, the United States must become a nation that saves and invests instead of spends.

A nation's total economic output is either consumed or invested. The preferred scenario assumes that 16 percent of GNP will be invested in the private sector. Federal, state, and local government spending for goods produced and services rendered would account for 20 percent of the gross national product (this would not include government spending on welfare, Social Security, and other similar "transfer payments"). Investment provides for future consumption: a certain level of investment is needed simply to maintain a stable output. In the last half of the 1970s, private investment in the GNP was barely 14 percent, and government spending reached 23 percent. When transfer payments are included in the calculations, total spending by all government levels has recently been about 35 percent of GNP. The federal share of this figure, including grants to the states, has been about 25 percent of GNP.

Why has investment been only 14 percent? Savings, the source of investment dollars, declined. The baby-boom generation came of age, found jobs, started families, and substantially increased the number of young adults. And young adults are vigorous consumers and borrowers. At the same time, inflation boosted prices, which lowered the net value of interest earned. The spiraling cost of energy itself rendered much existing equipment obsolete. Moreover, some investments were unproductive from an economic standpoint. Stringent environmental regulations required investor-owned businesses to purchase equipment that produces clean air and water but in itself does not produce marketable goods.

Economic planners and politicians increasingly have questioned the Keynesian theories of deficit finance. Easy money, low taxes, and more government spending boosted employment but also raised prices. Tight money, higher taxes, and reduced spending blunted inflation but increased unemployment. Policies designed to encourage consumption more often than not also discouraged investment. The growth of government spending at state, local, and national levels absorbed funds that otherwise might have been invested.

Private investment and government spending, unlike Peter Pan and Wendy, cannot fly together. Everything the city, state, and federal governments spend comes from their citizens. Government spends money in four ways: it buys products, it pays its employees, it pays the interest on the national debt, and it distributes transfer payments to recipients ranging from the needy to suburban transit systems. In the preferred scenario, citizens limit government spending at all levels (not inlcuding transfer payments) to 20 percent of GNP by 1990.

Productivity also depends on *how* government spends its tax dollars. The federal government takes 24 cents of every dollar a taxpayer earns. State and local governments take another 13 cents. The combined government take is virtually two dollars out of every five its citizens earn. With the two dollars, government spends 50 cents to buy what it needs—airplanes or school buildings, for example; it spends another 50 cents to pay its FBI investigators, mail carriers, and other employees; and it transfers the remaining dollar to other individuals through Social Security, pensions, grants, and so on. When the government buys capital improvements, it helps the economy, provided it does not buy too many. Economic growth and productivity require expenditures on roads, sewers, and public buildings as the nation's enterprise expands. In recent years the nation has been skimping on such spending in favor of transfer payments and most recently military equipment.

In the future, government spending must grow at a slower rate than the GNP, which would be a marked departure from the last 30 years when government expenditures rose at annual rates of 9.6 percent while the GNP averaged 7.5 percent.

Capital investment for the environment amounted to $16 billion in 1981. The preferred scenario assumes this investment will increase 3 percent annually, given moderate economic growth. If there is no growth, the environment may well worsen because we will not feel able to repair, improve, or save it. Since World War II, U.S. citizens have become more and more concerned with the environment. Over the years this concern swelled into an irresistible public pressure. The public, aware that some debilitating illnesses and diseases were man-made, wanted controls on the mercury levels in swordfish, on the manufacture of asbestos and food coloring, and on many other products that endangered health.

By the end of the 1960s, the federal government had passed

36 / PATHWAYS TO PROSPERITY

the Wilderness Act of 1963, the Clean Air and Water Act of 1965, the Clear Water Restoration Act of 1966, the Air Quality Act of 1967, and the National Environmental Policy Act of 1969.

As U.S. productivity and economic growth have slackened, the public has asked for a second look at the cost of environmental protection and cleanup. Some government environmental rules seem to produce little protection in proportion to the amount of regulation. Clearly, a balance needs to be struck; the world must use its environmental resources, but it must manage that exploitation wisely and with a view to the long term.

BUT WE WILL STILL PAY TAXES

Reducing government spending in favor of building up productive private investment starts with cutting taxes. Achieving the preferred path assumes that citizens gradually will reduce the personal income tax rate from 25 percent in 1980 to 11 percent in 1990. The savings and investment that will flow from these cuts will increase economic activity, which, in turn, will provide the government with adequate income and reduce the need for some current government spending on transfer payments.

The 46 percent rate that corporations pay should drop to 20 percent in 1990. Increasing the investment tax credit also promotes the goal of a 3 percent annual growth in GNP. The thrust of these choices is not to get more money in circulation but to get money into an industrial garden where it will fertilize verdant growth. Experience proves that 70 percent or more of this growth will be harvested by labor in the form of work and jobs. Thirty percent will be harvested by capital. Much of the 30 percent will be replanted to assure growth in future years; the remainder will flow to the owners of the investment dollars among whom are pension fund recipients, small stockholders, and others who have accumulated funds they are willing to risk.

ENTER ENERGY

Our energy problems of the last decade have been among the most publicized and economically significant the United States has faced. Chance takes a hand in the last scene of the preferred scenario in the form of escalating world oil prices. World oil prices, rather than individual or government decisions, determine the use and cost of all energy. Between 1973 and 1980, the price of oil rose from $2 to $40 a barrel. Oil cannot command the same price increase over the next decade because no country can afford it. The decline in oil prices in 1983 and the apparent inability of the OPEC nations to act in concert is no assurance that the price of oil will level off for long. It would be folly to expect world oil prices to decline or even remain level over the long term.

In the preferred scenario, oil prices rise annually at 4 percent above inflation, an intentionally pessimistic rate. Assuming bad luck on the chance factors of international relations, the unknown size of the world's oil resources, and the pace of technological advance is prudent as well as plausible. In the period from now to the year 2000, any of these factors, especially the political unknowns, could work to breathe new life into OPEC. Even a single event such as the outbreak of military conflict in the Middle East could swing the balance. When living in precarious times, it is best to be prepared for the worst.

Coal prices are assumed to rise at 1 percent annually above inflation. As the price of oil rises, the price of coal will also rise but at a slower rate. Synfuels—synthetic fuels created from the same chemical building blocks, hydrogen and carbon, that form petroleum and natural gas—are drawn from rocks, coal, and even sugar cane. But they, too, are expensive—considerably more expensive at the present time than an equivalent amount of energy output from oil.

Inflation and interest rates insure that by 2000 synfuels will still cost as much or more per barrel as oil. But they will be worth the money if they can relieve the oil demand. The United States consumes a minimal amount of synfuels now. In the preferred scenario, by the end of the century the United States will consume a much more significant amount.

To synfuel consumption must be added another 5 quads from solar energy. If we could capture all the energy that reaches earth from the sun in one day, we could meet the world's energy needs for a year. But that would entail covering the earth with solar collectors. Solar energy is highly diffuse. To make it useful, engineers must collect, concentrate, store, and convert it into other usable forms. While sunlight is free, the equipment is costly. The Solar Energy

Research Institute (SERI) estimates the 60 percent capital and 40 percent labor cost for capturing solar energy at $10.6 million per trillion Btu. SERI's figure does not include the cost of backup capital and labor to insure distribution and generation. Just as with synfuels, a barrel equivalent of solar energy could cost as much in 2000 as a barrel of oil.

By that time the United States could conceivably rely much more heavily on nuclear power for its energy needs. Presently, the United States has 83 nuclear reactors licensed to operate. Fifty-nine more are under construction, and of these 27 could be on line by the end of 1983. At that point nuclear energy will move ahead of hydro power and natural gas and be second only to coal as a generator of electricity in the United States. In 1982 nuclear generators produced 12.5 percent of the nation's electricity.

Since 1972 97 reactors have been cancelled either due to utilities' tight financial problems or recession-induced lower demand. A shutdown of the 83 reactors with current operating licenses would force us to import millions of additional barrels of oil every day and would cost electric households billions of dollars a year in fuel charges alone. It would cost these housholds many more billions to build coal-generating power plants. Power from nuclear plants is less expensive than from coal-fired plants and much less expensive than from oil. If the high costs of alternatives persuade the United States to go ahead with nuclear power, the nation will still be in a precarious position. Only four firms manufactured nuclear reactors in 1976, and two of these firms have ceased this manufacture as of 1981. If one more abandons production, there is no chance that the remaining firm could produce enough reactors to fill the need. And if we leave only one manufacturer, we eliminate the competitive market that spurs technology.

LIVING ON THE PREFERRED PATH

Quantitative scenarios by themselves principally interest economic modelers and planners. The rest of humanity tends to appreciate plot, color, detail, and chronology—the drama of narrative. By tracing the experiences of several fictional characters, we can illustrate what life would be like in the preferred scenario through the year 2000.

In microcosm these make-believe characters represent the life and work of many U.S. citizens. The average worker changes jobs six times, for example, but for the sake of convenience and simplicity, these workers remain employed relatively steadily. The important things about them are that they take risks and respond to opportunities made possible by the policy choices of their fellow citizens. They have a positive and hopeful outlook, and they are willing to change. They both shape and are shaped by the preferred path.

The first worker, Edward Bell, was hired by the Philadelphia Telephone Company in 1982 at age 21 as a lineman. After high school Bell served a three-year hitch in the army where he trained in communications. As soon as he was mustered out, he married and is now the proud father of a six-month-old son. Ed Bell is a family man: he loves his wife and his son; he reverently and punctually attends Our Lady of the Rosary Roman Catholic Church; and he looks forward expectantly to family gatherings with his brothers, parents, and cousins. He loves his work, having been attracted to it by the entry-level pay of $11,000, by the prospects of advancement through company training programs, and by the romantic image of the man on the telephone pole as a hero. His vision of the future is a matrix of family, friends, work, and church.

Dolores Martinez, 27, is a graduate of Northwestern University with a degree in systems research and marketing. She works for a La Salle Street advertising agency in the Chicago Loop where she earns $27,000 a year and does advanced work in computer applications to market analysis. She goes to dinner, the theatre, and to art museums with an enthusiastic office space salesman with whom she wants to live. Soon they get married.

Townsend Bullitt is a 42-year-old publisher. He issues a newsletter once a month that lists every appropriation passed by town, city, or state for the construction of schools, hospitals, police facilities, town halls, and the like. He markets this list to concrete, steel, lumber, and aluminum manufacturers and to construction firms. He must devote 10 to 12 hours a day to compiling the appropriation information and still finds the time to advertise to attract potential subscribers. In addition to his newsletter activity, he teaches part-time at the University of Denver. His teaching stipend is the one firm element of his income. Rising postal rates seriously affect his business. The recession cuts into the discretionary money corporations will pay for his information. Sometimes Bullitt is hard-pressed to meet the salaries of his three employees. But he sees a promising future for his business, especially if he can publish an international edition.

Ed Bell works hard and steadily to support his family, for it is through them that he finds his satisfaction. Dolores Martinez marries and pursues the career for which she trained. Townsend Bullitt works in his own business. He knows that he has the chance to make a large profit, and he is willing to take the risk of a loss. As an entrepreneur, he is part of a burgeoning growth of small businesses providing information and services. He has some advantages not available to the others. His car, for example, which his company owns, is a deductible expense, as are his travel and most entertainment.

In mid 1982 each of these workers received a tax cut and had to decide what to do with the money. Ed Bell has an extra $300. Spend it or save it? Go to Atlantic City or pay off the car? Bell chooses to pay off the car, a way of saving. He spares himself interest payments.

Dolores receives $800; her husband an equal amount. At this juncture in their lives, the advertising agency for which she works issues stock. Dolores and her husband buy ten shares for $1,600. They realize, of course, that this money may be tied up for an appreciable length of time since it is an unlisted stock and may not be marketable. But both of them are privy to information about the growth of the marketing industry and both are confident. They reason that the life of most publicly held corporations is usually long and that investment in a new venture can appreciate rapidly, although the risk of loss is greater. Steadily employed, these two willingly assume this risk.

Townsend Bullitt receives a tax break of $2,000 to which he adds another $3,000 to hire stringers in Mexico and Brazil whose reports enable him to issue a modest international edition.

In the aggregate these three choose to save and invest. The tax cut makes this possible. Liberalized investment tax laws make saving and investing attractive. Multiplied by working men and women throughout the country, a process of stable, moderate, long-term growth is initiated in this way. Because Bell, Martinez, and Bullitt limit their spending, they keep prices down.

In 1984, as the economy gains momentum, the three receive another modest tax cut and this time bank their savings. They bank because there are goods and services they want over the longer term.

Ed Bell and his wife want another child. They save for the obstetrician, the pediatrician, the hospital, the Pampers, and the Enfamil. Dolores and her husband bank their savings while trying to decide whether to invest in a rental condominium in Florida or to buy a house in the suburbs. No matter which they buy, they can deduct taxes and mortgage interest. If they buy the condo, they can depreciate its value, a tax break, as well as deduct the cost of maintenance. But they are not assured that the rent they will receive will always cover costs. If they buy a house, they may gain a greater degree of equity sooner, and they will have the benefits of owning their own shelter. Bullitt invests his tax savings in a Keogh account, which he has established as a self-employed worker. All have entrusted their savings to the money market, which converts savings into productive investment.

In 1986 there is a down cycle, as well as greater inflation, caused in part by the final decontrol of natural gas prices. Oil prices rise, too, as the recovering U.S. and European economies consume the glut of 1982–83. The three workers feel it. They moderate their travel, insulate their homes, and conserve wherever possible. They grumble from time to time, but underneath they are basically optimistic about their futures.

Ed Bell prospers with the flowering of the information economy and the growth of telecommunications technology. Thousands of firms respond to new technologies developed by the telephone companies, and Ed Bell, smart and ready to learn, moves up to foreman as a skilled and expert technician.

Many firms that market data and information services compete. As competition intensifies, more and more firms report to advertising. Dolores Martinez designs an original program to do marketing analysis of information services.

Bullitt had accurately gauged the future of his business. He borrows and cashes in savings to enlarge his firm. He hires more stringers, installs a new computer, and, when forced to rent more office space, decides to build his own office building. There is a degree of prestige as well as a certain security in owning his building. But the tax laws are decisive. Bullitt can take advantage of many write-offs and can depreciate the building over a period of 15 years. While the building is modest by modern standards, it still represents an additional $750,000 to the construction industry in Denver, and many contractors eagerly submit bids.

Bell, Martinez, and Bullitt are living through a transition. A government, it seems, always needs a core project to focus on one overpowering problem it must solve before moving on. In the 1930s, it was employment; in the 1940s, the war. In the 1960s and 1970s, the core project was social welfare, which peaked when financing faltered. The core project of the 1980s is investment to increase productivity and jobs. Our workers' ability and willingness to work and save for goals helps them and the economy. They, in turn, are helped by the reorientation of federal and state income tax systems. These reforms enrich the economy. For example, Ed Bell, a salaried worker, has a list of monthly necessities: his rent, food, a clothing allowance, a car to get to work. At the end of the month, there is usually little appreciable surplus. The hardest bite of all in Ed Bell's salary, the one bite he cannot defer because his employer deducts it, is his withholding tax. But the government indexes the personal income tax. It freezes "bracket creep," which automatically moves a worker into a new bracket because of inflationary salaries that do not amount to a true appreciation in buying power. When Ed Bell gets a raise, when his overtime is significant, he now has a surplus.

The government spurs Delores Martinez's savings and investment by insuring that she receives a competitive rate of return: it eliminates interest rate limits on passbook savings and increases the tax exclusion on dividend income. It spurs Townsend Bullitt by reducing corporate taxes if his earnings are invested in new facilities. It decreases the tax life on equipment and structures.

The government makes demands upon them, too, by cutting its own spending. The Bells have two sons, and they want a college education for both. They support the idea of a tax exemption for tuition payments, which would greatly facilitate this goal. The Bells listen carefully, however, when a member of Congress explains that a college education is not a constitutional right that the government must insure; that these exemptions will benefit a minority at the expense of a majority; that the government does offer some provisions for a college education, such as funding by the military in exchange for service or low-cost tuition loans, which the student can contract from leading institutions.

The government inconveniences Dolores Martinez when it refuses to subsidize an intersuburban transit system. Federal analysts argue cogently that suburban transit systems are properly the concern of suburbanites. These suburbanites must wrestle with the prospect of subsidizing such systems themselves. Steadily rising oil prices tip the balance in favor of transit systems.

The government also penalizes Townsend Bullitt—first, by raising postal rates annually and then by withdrawing in part from a vast building program of offices, military facilities, and dormitory accommodations. Its decision makes Bullitt's business more precarious at first because no town, city, or state can build with the gusto of the federal government. But towns, cities, and states still build, and the competition for contracts is keen. In the longer term there is more money available at lower interest rates to private developers, and overall construction goes up. The federal government itself shifts its own spending priorities to favor major capital improvements such as roads and bridges. Bullitt's newsletter increases in value.

Inflation never drops to zero, but during the period through 2000 it advances only between 5 and 6 percent, which is manageable. Still, by the late 1990s gasoline costs $3.00 a gallon, and electricity rates are more than double what they were in 1980. In response to the incessant rise in oil prices, the government makes a commitment to nuclear-generating power. Government and industry respond to public concern about the potential danger of nuclear power by maintaining strict standards and conducting a public education program to provide people with technical and economic facts. The government installs nuclear waste storage systems capable of disposing of wastes accumulated over a long period of time. The successful experience of France and Japan with nuclear power also encourage the U.S. effort.

There are bad times for some along the way. In 1990 energy prices soar because a border war between Middle Eastern countries cuts off oil supplies for three months. The transfer of manufacturing and industry to third world countries continues because labor and materials are cheaper there. As a consequence, large contingents of U.S. workers retrain for employment in the information, service, and specialized manufacturing industries. It is a crucial trial for the country and a painful trial for these employees. Masses of workers move from the Great Lakes states to the Sun Belt where food processing requires more and more hands to help fill the world demand. Other workers go to New England where electronics and software companies keep proliferating.

In his environment Ed Bell wants a fish-filled Pocono Mountain stream, supervised playgrounds for his kids, and a litter-free street.

Dolores Martinez worries about air and noise pollution in Chicago. Townsend Bullitt believes that coal-burning plants must "scrub" their waste so that no more than 2.5 percent effluent escapes. To Bullitt the cost of cleaning coal to an absolute degree is unbearable for the consumer; so he sees no reason why a plant that burns coal with a lower effluent must scrub.

In two decades, the U.S. economy makes substantial progress in environmental protection because industry has the surplus to make this investment. Industry increases its investment in preserving air, land, and water by 3 percent per year. Steady economic growth brings a rapid turnover in plant and equipment. And new plants accommodate advanced antipollutant measures and devices at less cost than old.

By the 1900s progress has been made in checking the deterioration of public facilities such as bridges, roads, sewers, water systems, parks, and schools. Government gives priority to investments shoring up these splits and crevices, and this repair promotes access and convenience, both of which help business growth. Public capital investment also means jobs, and jobs create tax revenues.

The underprivileged poor do not disappear. They are always there for a variety of reasons, despite altruistic attempts to alleviate their plight. The progress charted by Ed Bell, Delores Martinez, and Townsend Bullitt does not relieve or remedy the lot of the poor, but economic progress means there are fewer underprivileged because many are absorbed within the labor force. When welfare is no longer competitive with employment, many will work. And as they go to work, the gap between upper and lower incomes narrows. The poor on occasion do become rich just as the rich on occasion become poor.

Bell, Martinez, and Bullitt delayed their consumption in 1982. Their minor abstinence may seem at first an unimpressive gesture, but, in examining the usual mix of 10 percent savings to 90 percent consumption, the shift of one percentage point has an effect out of all proportion to its weight. If savings increase by 1 percent and consumption decreases by 1 percent, billions of dollars are put to productive purposes.

Ed Bell is nearly 40 years old in 2000, a supervisor of skilled technicians, making more than $30,000 a year. He has reached the peak of his potential earnings, but his earnings will continue at this level for another 20 years and perhaps longer. At 44 years of age, Dolores Martinez is the executive vice-president of her agency. She has helped guide her firm into international marketing, the profits from which are huge. Her income still mounts. Bullitt's firm merges with a conglomerate, and Townsend can live well on the dividends his stock pays, let alone his salary as vice-president.

These three individuals have led what can only be described as productive, successful, and prosperous lives. They have contributed to a stable economy, which sometimes staggered but always recovered. Their contributions, of course, worked to their nation's as well as their own interests.

But what about those who did not have the initial advantage of training, intelligence, foresight, and opportunity? Leon Joe Matthews, a fourth character in the preferred scenario, offers a perspective on this question. Leon is born out of wedlock in 1970 in Detroit. The youngest of four children, Leon never knows his father. His infancy is sustained by Aid to Dependent Children, which barely provides his mother with the means to feed him.

Leon is barely literate. Yet the schools routinely pass him along from one grade to the next. School work never claims his attention because he only fitfully perceives what is taught. Bored and confused, he takes to the streets early. By 10 he knows that drugs are an important part of life. The men who buy and sell drugs are the men who count in Leon's world. At 16 Leon is arrested for petty theft. A juvenile court judge offers him the choice between a spell in a reformatory or going to work. A probation officer finds a job for Leon as a counter clerk in a fast-food franchise. In two years Leon advances to become supervisor of his shift. His company finances his education in a supervisory training program for two months. Another two years of experience and training enable him to get a job with a food service company that supplies provisions to large institutions. As he reaches adulthood, Leon has learned that there is work and that it is possible to rely on the economy. His advancement is not fast and his salary increments are small, but they are steady and therefore in sync with the economy.

By 1995 Leon's income is such to encourage marriage and allow him to rent an apartment. Out from under the pressures of subsistence living, his life is not the world's most affluent, but neither is it mean and spiritless.

These lives transpire in the preferred scenario, a future that is both plausible and achievable. It is a path that presents its own set of sacrifices and rewards.

In a low-growth scenario, Ed Bell will have made less money. Though his salary increases, it is eroded by inflation. And he will have remained a lineman. After twenty years of low growth, Ed will still be an employee but not a supervisor, because improvements and innovations will not have taken place as quickly. He is stuck in his job, and it will have robbed him of the confidence he needs to enlarge his family.

Because of the sluggish economy, advertising billings vacillate. Delores Martinez changes jobs in 1984 and again in 1988. She works gainfully but always with the advertising representative's apprehension that one day she will not get the next job because she will be too old or burned out.

Townsend Bullitt's newsletter succeeds in its way, but its success is always erratic and episodic. Bullitt holds on to his position at the university, never quite optimistic enough to let go. In the year 2000 Bullitt moves into modest faculty housing when he decides to sell his business and teach full-time.

Leon Joe Matthews gets several jobs, but he cannot keep any of them long enough to gain the experience and confidence he needs. He works in fast-food restaurants when he can; when this is impossible, he steals purses and cars or burglarizes houses. While he is never addicted, drugs play an important role in his life. He is never sure enough of his future to marry, although he does father children. No chain ever offers him training because no chain ever has the surplus to afford these programs. Leon never escapes a dependence on social welfare, which has to support his illegitimate children.

Obviously, the low-growth economy these four people populate is unstable. It fluctuates between stagnant and inflationary cycles, declining capital investment, continued dependence on government social welfare programs, continued unemployment, poor labor productivity, sporadic innovation, and high energy prices.

Social fragmentation and a pervasive hopelessness become institutionalized irritants. The birth rate does not reach replacement level, and immigration never exceeds the quota. The labor force sees fewer women participate, and more men retire early. Labor productivity grows at only 1.23 percent annually, and investment as a percentage of the GNP is lower. While investment in environmental protection still grows at 3 percent, it is 3 percent of a lower base. Personal income taxes go up, but actual tax revenue is less. Investment incentives are paltry. Tax credits and depreciation rates do not change; therefore, they do not prompt investment. Energy prices never stop rising, thereby fanning inflation. While alternate energy sources develop, they are slower in coming. This is not a scenario that offers prosperity, and its portrait of survival is hardly encouraging.

The most compelling argument for establishing policies that lead to the preferred scenario, therefore, is the quality of life that it offers—a qulaity of life that stands out even more when juxtaposed with the comparatively mean life U.S. citizens would face under lower-growth conditions. The U.S. economy will not improve dramatically until productivity rates increase, and such increases depend on increased savings and investment. A scenario described in terms of its equations remains a series of abstractions, but couched as the context for a series of biographies such as those presented here, it becomes a convincing argument for the preferred scenario's level of economic growth.

LOOKING BOTH WAYS

Loren Eiseley has suggested that there are two different pairs of spectacles through which philosophers may look at the world. "Through one we see ourselves in the light of the past; through the other, in the light of the future. If we fail to use both pairs of spectacles equally, our view of ourselves and of the world is apt to be distorted, since we can never be completely without the use of both."*

Our fictitious characters have provided a window on a possible future. In Chapter 5 we profile some flesh-and-blood people who by their personal lives provide windows on the past and present.

---

*Loren Eiseley, *The Unexpected University* (New York: Harcourt, Brace & World, 1969), p. 125.

4
Policy Choices for the Information Age

The economic problems confronting our economy, as well as those caused by resource depletion, environmental pollution, and the arms race, are the products of past choices; their solutions lie in choices available to us now and in the future. Constructing scenarios helps us envision potential futures so that in choosing the one we would most like to realize, we can fashion national policies designed to guide us to our destination. The options inherent in the preferred scenario, as well as the protection it offers the United States' hard-won standard of living, clearly make it the most advantageous future this nation could seek. Defining those policies best fitted to yielding that scenario, therefore, is the principal goal of this book, just as instituting them should be the priority of all U.S. citizens for whom survival is synonymous with success in achieving prosperity. The recommendations advanced here are not limited to public or government policies. They concern private business, labor unions, and volunteer organizations as well.

Every age faces a unique set of challenges and a seemingly insurmountable set of problems. Not surprisingly, the periods of transition from one era to another provide the most stress and the most uncertainty and, at the same time, the greatest opportunities. The 1980s are such a transition period for the United States. Our economy is in the advanced stages of a shift from an industrial to an information base. This fundamental change may provide solutions to many of the problems that have crippled U.S. productivity and economic growth in the past two decades.

THE INFORMATION ECONOMY

In the industrial age, resources and capital served as the basic elements of production. In the postindustrial, information age, these elements have been replaced by information and knowledge. Few realize the degree to which the shift to this kind of economy already has occurred. Industries such as computers, communications, entertainment, finance, "government," and education and training have founded a new type of economy so successfully that the information worker now dominates the United States' labor force. Indeed, the information sector has grown from less than 20 percent of the labor force in 1950 to over 50 percent today, while the industrial sector has shrunk from nearly 40 percent of the total number of workers in 1950 to under 20 percent today. Of the nearly 20 million new jobs created in the 1970s, only 4 million were in manufacturing.

In 1950 more than 30 percent of the work force belonged to labor unions as opposed to less than 20 percent in 1980. Correspondingly, the political influence and bargaining power of unions has diminished. Labor's stronghold industries, such as steel, automobiles, and construction, now bargain about "take aways"—what wage and fringe benefits workers will cede.

The information economy has also supplanted the traditional power of national political parties with the power of mass media. Candidates are marketed directly to the public through television and newspapers, which makes the party machinery less crucial to political figures than space in newspapers and radio and television advertising.

The lifeblood of the information economy is advanced communications technology built on a framework of solid state microchips. Made from silicon—the main ingredient of sand—microchips are the tiny building blocks of all computing devices, from little pocket calculators to giant industrial robots. Their potential is truly staggering. Various kinds of industrial robots, for example, will soon be performing many of the strictly mechanical tasks associated with assembly line production. As a result, large numbers of workers will be freed from repetitive and boring mechanical tasks and offered the option of upgrading the quality of their work life by learning new skills. The need for retraining and basic education is enormous in scope.

Meanwhile, applications for the tiny silicon microprocessor chips keep multiplying. Microprocessors are shrinking in size, doing their work faster, and becoming constantly cheaper—all at exponential rates. Christopher Evans, author of *The Micro Millenium*, illustrates these changes in computers with a delightful comparison: "If the Rolls Royce had changed comparably since World War II, it would now cost $2.75, get 3 million miles per gallon, and six of them would fit on the head of a pin."*

Datamation magazine predicts that large-scale computers now used by business will go the way of the dinosaurs. By 1990, according to the magazine, "the industry may be seeing the last hurrah of the last generation of big centralized corporate mainframes. Advances in microchip technology and software will make it much cheaper and easier to use desktop computers interlinked with a network of other terminals."†

Growing shortages of microprocessor chips are worrying some countries. Maintaining an adequate level of electronics capability is a matter of strategic importance. A dependency on foreign semiconductor chips may become as important as a dependency on foreign oil suppliers.

Advanced information and communications technologies are also influencing energy use patterns and the situations that lead to environmental pollution in highly positive ways. The new economy is much less energy-, materials-, and transportation-intensive. Thus the environmental and resource problems associated with these factors can be reduced greatly. Information is an inexhaustible resource.

As proof that increased information can help to conserve energy, the American Telephone and Telegraph Company and Duke Power Company have begun a large-scale test of electronic home energy management systems in one thousand homes in Charlotte, North

---

*Christopher Evans, *The Micro Millenium* (New York: Washington Press, 1981), p. 77.
†*Technology Forecasts*, newsletter, Los Angeles, June 1982, p. 2.

Carolina. They have connected microprocessors to television sets to display weather information, daily energy messages, and constantly updated energy usage figures. Customers can program and operate their major appliances by remote control. AT&T and Duke Power estimate that such a sustem can reduce an individual family's utility costs by 20 percent.

Duke Power also has offered customers cash incentives to install wire systems that connect major home appliances directly to the utility company; by allowing the utility company to shut off the appliances for short periods during peak demand periods, the customers are involved in a cooperative plan to reduce peak load, which makes it unnecessary to build as much new generating capacity as otherwise would be required. Duke Power estimates that by 1990 direct load management will eliminate the need for more than $10 billion in new plant construction. Such tremendous savings ultimately reduce the consumers' bills. Computers also make possible enormous cost efficiencies through electronic monitoring of electricity use, automatic meter reading, billing, and collecting. Technology like this amounts to increased productivity, with services being rendered at a fraction of present costs.

Four events in 1981 point to the fact that the information economy is the predominant emerging economic trend of our time. One, the largest corporation in the world, American Telephone and Telegraph Company, agreed to divest itself of its operating regional telephone companies in order to compete on an unregulated basis in the high technology areas of information and communication; two, Piedmont Natural Gas, a North Carolina utility, moved into the cable television business; three, Sears Roebuck introduced TELE-SHOP, its first optical video disc catalog of 18,000 products; and, four, IBM began marketing its first personal computer.

These developments underscore one important characteristic of the emerging information society—its diversity. In the fields of communication and home entertainment, network television has dominated the last 30 years, dictating what programs the public watches. Cable television provides a more diverse information flow; the uniformities of "mass culture" are giving way to a range of artistic expression and public information of greater variety.

Clearly, to meet the needs of the information society, schools and education will have to change dramatically. "Teaching machines" will affect pupil-teacher interaction in the classroom, but this development is only the tip of the iceberg. With the advent of computer access to up-to-date worldwide data bases on virtually every subject, students can assert more responsibility for their own learning. Not only can students study and learn at their own pace at their own computer terminal, there is no practical limit on the amount of knowledge to which any student can have access.

Office work is also being transformed. Many secretaries no longer type letters at a typewriter and file copies in filing cabinets. Sitting at terminals with keyboards, secretaries "enter" letters or memos, make all necessary corrections on-line and send the text to a supervisor's viewing screen for approval. The document then can be sent to a recipient's terminal screen in the same building or across the country, or a "hard copy" (paper copy) can be printed for mailing. Copies of the letter are stored automatically in computer files to be retrieved when needed at the push of a button.

Many computer services already are a reality, and many more will be realized in the years ahead, but our understanding of the significance of the computer age is probably still as rudimentary as was that of turn-of-the-century observers of the telephone. People simply were unable to perceive what the ability to link people instantaneously all over the world would mean; looking at the small instrument, they could not imagine the power of the future communications network.

The home computer revolution is at least equal in importance to the invention of the printing press and the Industrial Revolution. The implications of the invention of the printing press offer a concrete example of the degree of social change triggered by a new technology. In the Middle Ages, the production of books and reading material was a monopoly held by the clergy. In fact, the clergy were virtually the only members of the population who could read. Each book was produced by hand lettering on vellum pages, and only books of religious value, like the Bible, were reproduced. It was a slow and paintstaking process; only a few books were produced, which made them very rare. They were distributed to churches where they were read aloud at weekly services. The invention of the printing press theoretically gave everyone access to the written word. In a matter of a few generations, what was once a largely illiterate population had begun to teach each other to read. Once people could read, they began exchanging all sorts of information—without the church serving as an intermediary. The exchange of ideas blossomed, which in turn led to increased public awareness of the social issues of the time. This process indirectly produced the intellectual climate that fostered the Renaissance.

A generation of youth (the "on-line generation") currently is growing up with computers and therefore has a revolutionary way of learning, thinking, and communicating. Teenagers, who might begin with a disturbing addiction to video games, are graduating to programming the games and, from that, to a consuming interest in the use of computers for all kinds of purposes.

Recent developments in the financial community provide an even more convincing example of the way the information revolution has transformed things: Merrill Lynch now has 500,000 investors enrolled in a cash management program that allows small investors to move money from one account to another electronically. They have also entered the money market fund business and sponsor their own VISA card. Sears Roebuck has acquired Dean Witter Reynolds, Inc., the sixth largest U.S. stock brokerage. Sears also has plans to open its own money market account.

American Express has acquired not only the brokerage firm of Shearson Hammill but also a cable television company that provides customers a two-way interactive system for shopping, financial transactions, and entertainment. In the traditional world of finance, banks were curtailed by a heavy burden of federal regulation that spelled out the interest rates to be charged on loans and to be paid on savings. Savers have channeled their savings into unregulated money market accounts, like those sponsored by Merrill Lynch, which are not subject to regulations applied to banks. From all appearances, the information society already has helped transform the financial market.

The computer revolution not only promises to revolutionize our business as well as our social lives; it also offers the potential to boost the individual worker's productivity and therefore, by extrapolation, the productivity of the nation. But being offered the means to rejuvenate a flagging economy and exploiting its potential are not necessarily synonymous. A firm national commitment to increasing the rates of productivity growth is essential. Without reasonably robust productivity growth, it will be difficult—if not impossible—to stop inflation, improve the lot of the poor, continue improving the environment, compete in international trade, and maintain a satisfactory level of defense. Improving productivity is key to realizing the preferred future with its desirable economic and social benefits. Productivity growth requires the understanding and cooperation of business, labor, and government. Cooperation in all social and economic spheres will reduce the need for government-imposed sanctions.

PRODUCTIVITY AND WORK

Labor productivity growth provides a convenient index to the nation's economic well-being. The preferred scenario seeks an annual rate of growth in labor productivity of about 2.2 percent, compared to the historic high of 2.9 percent from 1960-69 and the historic low of 1.2 percent from 1969-78.

In the information economy, the sources of productivity improvement and the nature of work itself will be substantially changed. Productivity advances will have to come in large measure from white-collar workers, who now account for the bulk of the labor force. In addition to dominating the nation's worker pool, white-collar workers are also the fastest growing segment of a company's ever-increasing payroll; even in large manufacturing companies, a half or more of the firm's payroll dollars now goes to white-collar workers. Management consultant Dennis Callaghan predicts that the proportion of spending for white-collar work will continue to rise in the future. Studies by Callaghan and his associates have determined that the average white-collar worker is about 10 percent less productive than the average blue-collar worker, who is productive about 55 percent of the time.*

William Saffady, the author of *The Automated Office: An Introduction to the Technology*, believes that automated office systems are the primary factor in technological change—the dominant force in productivity improvement generally and the critical element in improved white collar productivity. Citing the changes in the composition of the American work force, he concludes that improvements

---

Technology Forecasts, newsletter, Los Angeles, October 1981, p. 5.

in office productivity are essential to the continued growth of our national economy.*

The emergence of the information economy raises deeper questions about work, unemployment, and compensation. During the years of affluence, when the manufacturing economy came to full bloom, wage levels rose steadily. Higher wages inevitably lead to the search for alternatives to labor. It is a common misconception that unemployment is caused by technological progress. It is social and economic developments that drive technology, not the other way around. Without rising wages, much new technology would have remained theories or stayed in the laboratories of pure science. The application of technical innovations occurs because it is cheaper in the long run than human labor. As long as labor continues to get more expensive, so-called technological unemployment will increase.

In the information economy, work (in the traditional sense of work meaning labor) is disappearing. People are spending less and less time at "work." The decline of the work week described as one element of the preferred scenario is only one part of the process. Longer vacations, more holidays, and earlier retirement add to the trend. A major factor in the new context is longer education and training periods.

The habitual political response to unemployment, that is, government jobs programs, is both a symptom of the disappearance of jobs and an illustration of how old solutions will no longer work. Underemployment—the "occupying" of people in useless activities as a substitute for welfare—is degrading and ultimately does more damage than good to the individual and the society.

As the microelectronics revolution proceeds, it will touch far more than repetitious factory jobs. There are designs and prototypes for robotic medical consultants and legal advisors as well as automated factories.

The decline of work raises profound and yet unanswered questions about the nature of society. How will society be structured without the discipline of work? How will wealth or even basic necessities be distributed if not in exchange for labor?

---

*William Saffady, *The Automated Office: An Introduction to the Technology* (Silver Spring, Md.: 1981 National Micrographics Association).

These are the forces underlying the enormous growth in new small businesses. The great majority of new jobs are in activities that did not exist a few years ago. In 1950 the Census Bureau survey of occupations had 270 categories; in 1980 it has 503. We are creating new kinds of work, much of which is self-employing and ulitmately more satisfying and rewarding than the more traditional occupations.

LABOR PAINS

Changes in the economic base and the nature of work demand major adjustments on the part of labor unions. Not only is the total number of workers in unions declining because service and information industries are hard to organize, but unions are in trouble in their old power base—the manufacturing industries. Rapidly changing markets require fast product changes and flexible job assignments. This is difficult under traditional union rules with strict job definitions. The narrow specializations probably contributed to productivity in old-style mass production processes, but with today's highly segmented markets that is no longer the case. High wages are no longer managers' principal objection to unions. In fact, they are willing to pay more to avoid union-imposed rigid work rules. Labor unions are going to have to make major adjustments to increase flexibility on the shop floor if they are to survive.

RETHINKING EDUCATION

The skill requirements of the new marketplace are changing so rapidly that massive education and retraining of people are essential. A fundamental reorientation of the philosophy of education will also be necessary. In the past once workers were trained in their jobs, they rarely needed to acquire new skills. But in the information economy, workers can expect a continuing emphasis on new training and new abilities and on the value of continuing education.

Although the United States began the revolution in information technology, other countries have adjusted better to its educational requirements. Japan, West Germany, and the Soviet Union all offer their high school students more rigorous and advanced math and science curricula that better prepare them for roles in a highly technological economy than does the United States. This long-term investment in education has paid off particularly well for Japan, where the national mean IQ score has jumped more than seven points in a single generation. According to a study reported in the British journal *Nature*, this places young Japanese more than ten points higher than their counterparts in the United States and Europe. Richard Lynn, a psychologist and author of the report, concluded, "Since intelligence is a determinant of economic success, as it is of success in many other fields, the Japanese IQ advantage may have been a significant factor in Japan's outstandingly higher rate of economic growth."*

It is not as though the United States has not spent enough on public education in the past. After the launching of Sputnik in 1957, the U.S. government made a grand investment in education and has spent handsomely over the years. In 1973 the United States spent more on education than any other country: 7.7 percent of gross national product compared to 4.4 percent for Sweden, the runner-up. In March of 1983 the House of Representatives adopted a five-year, $1.1 billion bill to improve math and science education.

Public spending, however, has not translated into quality education in the United States. In fact, the results have been shockingly poor. Twenty percent of adults in the United States are functionally illiterate. Barbara Lerner has reported on the results of standardized tests administered in secondary schools in 21 countries in the 1960s and 1970s. On 19 tests ranging from reading comprehension to chemistry, U.S. students as a group scored last three times. In no category did they score first or second. Overall, the U.S. scores were closer to Thailand's than any of the developed countries.†

In the 1980s the private sector of the information economy will have to take a larger role in the funding and renewal of education. It will be a matter of self-preservation in the international market. The price of education and retraining will be high for business and individuals alike, but the price of ignorance and not having market-

---

*Richard Lynn, article in *Nature*, May 20, 1982, as reported in the *Washington Post*, June 13, 1982, p. A14.
†Barbara Lerner, "American Education: How Are We Doing?" *The Public Interest*, Fall 1982.

able skills will be higher. In 1981 U.S. firms spent $3,000 per worker on new equipment, but only $300 for on-the-job training. The application-oriented private sector is the most fruitful setting for retraining.

One avenue for business support of basic education is the well-established approach of direct contributions to public schools. In 1980 corporate donations to education passed $1 billion. The Bank of America gives $1 million a year to schools in California. The Allegheny Conference, a business group in Pennsylvania, contributes a similar amount in that state.

Business can assist in reorienting curricula to emphasize skills with expanding possibilities. Forty percent of all jobs now require a basic technical background. Programs must offer strong incentives, not the least of which is assured employment, the most attractive incentive of all. Government can provide incentives for individuals and businesses in this area. Such incentives could include low interest loans for adult vocational education and tax credits to businesses for spending on training and education. There is a total of 12 federal jobs-training programs now in existence. All of them will come up for renewal by 1984. The timing could not be better for a total revision of U.S. job-training and education policies.

Business also needs to examine closely management practices, labor constraints, and government's impact on the productive process. The United States seems to have ignored or forgotten much of what it earlier taught the West Germans and Japanese about entrepreneurship, management, quality control, work simplification, and worker incentives; thus we need to analyze the practices of foreign competitors.

THE POSITIVE ROLE OF GOVERNMENT

Productivity improvement will be facilitated greatly by a shared vision—a common purpose. Generating that vision should be the central role of government. At present, government's role tends to be negative, focusing on regulation, restraint, and rigidity. Prosperity, indeed survival, requires that government assume a positive role by articulating national goals and inspiring all U.S. citizens to combine their efforts to achieve them.

The space program, which was initiated at the beginning of the

1960s, illustrates government at its best. Putting men on the moon was a dramatic accomplishment with many practical economic benefits: our information economy and advanced telecommunications technology are to a large degree the result of investments made in the U.S. space program. The urgent need for lighter payloads in space, for example, produced the microminiaturization of data-processing equipment. Such developments underscore the belief in a real relationship between a strong space program, the state of U.S. science and technology, and the economic and psychological health of the nation.

Total research and development spending for all purposes has dropped from nearly 3 percent of the GNP in the mid-1960s to barely 2.2 percent in the late 1970s, with most of the decline occurring in federally funded research. The private sector increased its investment in research and development by 7 percent in 1981. Government spending on research and development has shifted markedly from long-term basic research to short-term responses to environmental and other regulatory restrictions. With severe limitations on government research and development money, the emphasis should shift back to long-term basic research, which will work to improve national productivity.

POLICY CHOICES TO PROMOTE SAVING AND INVESTMENT

The preferred scenario calls for raising the real investment growth rate to at least 3.5 percent per year until the year 2000 ("real" means adjusted for inflation). We usually think of investments as choices exercised by individuals and businesses, but government policy can provide tremendous incentives and disincentives.

For example, stable regulatory and monetary policies encourage investment. In addition, reducing deficits will minimize government competition for investment funds, and reducing taxes on income from savings will encourage savings, not to mention the desire to work and to invest. Increasing the tax exclusion on dividend income would encourage savings, as would taxing income from savings separately from other income (primarily wages and salaries), with each segment taxed progressively after certain exclusions. Such methods are designed to encourage savings indirectly by increasing net after-tax income.

The government should insure that small savers get a competitive rate of return on their savings. In recent years government policy has aimed at removing restrictions on small savers at the same time that private institutions have developed new and attractive investment vehicles. This trend should continue and, in fact, accelerate: the interest rate limits on passbook savings should be promptly eliminated and returns on small-denomination government securities raised to competitive levels.

Inflation produces "bracket creep," with taxpayers facing automatic tax increases as they move into higher and higher tax brackets. Bracket creep has become a major source of federal revenues: individual income taxes rose from 11 percent of adjusted gross income in 1976 to 14 percent in 1980 and 15.2 percent in 1981 (barring tax decreases). The indexing measure adopted in 1981 to become effective in 1985 will be helpful in holding taxes down.

Both demand- and supply-side models have shown that increasing the rate of return on business investment is an effective way to increase capital spending. By decreasing the tax lives of productive structures and equipment (faster depreciation rates), the government has boosted incentives for investment. This move will be as effective at the national level as a reduction in the corporate income tax, although it may be necessary to differentiate between capital-intensive manufacturing industries and labor-intensive service industries. Other options include increasing the investment tax credit and extending it to the modernization of old facilities, indexing depreciation accruals to offset the effects of inflation, reducing the capital gains tax, eliminating the double taxation of dividends, and allowing tax-free dividend investment.

CONTROLLING GOVERNMENT SPENDING

Incentives to increase savings and reduce consumer spending will help to hold down inflation. But government spending is still the greatest culprit in creating inflation. Inflation is rooted in the government-promoted illusion that you can have something for nothing— that you can spend more than you have by borrowing from future income. Government spending and deficits hit higher and higher levels starting with the Vietnam War and has continued into 1983, when the federal deficit was expected to be $210 billion. To finance the deficits incurred by the war and by vast social welfare programs, the federal government printed and circulated more money. Thus the value of money declined sharply in the 1970s—or, to put it another way, the cost of everything was inflated.

Inflation can be curbed by reducing government spending and borrowing. Cuts in federal spending are being made on the domestic side of the budget now, although it is a process that produces results slowly. But if federal deficits are to be reduced significantly, defense spending must also be cut sharply. Reducing the federal deficit will take time—four to five years—but it is the only way to reduce or remove the threat of inflation.

When the Federal Reserve Board placed sharp constraints on money supplies in 1981 to cut inflation, the economy went into a recession, which suggests that monetary policy alone will not serve as the sole cure for inflation. Moreover, this approach unfairly burdens the housing, automobile, and consumer durables industries. A balanced combination of reduced government spending and borrowing together with controls on money supply and credit will be required to restore economic growth and control inflation. The orientation of these policies must shift from concern about stimulating demand to concern about stimulating supply.

To prepare a program that restrains the growth of government spending, we need to review all current government activities periodically. Two questions must guide us: Can government clearly accomplish the activity more efficiently than a private sector institution could? Is the activity a legitimate responsibility of government? The legitimate responsibilities of government include national defense; protecting citizens from the illegal acts of other citizens; making rules for arbitrating contractual disputes; providing temporary, minimum subsistence to those unable to provide for themselves; and administering long-established government programs (e.g., Social Security), which cannot in a practical sense be turned over to private sector management. Efforts to restrain government spending should be concentrated initially on activities that fail or only marginally meet these criteria.

In 1981 the federal government started to reduce its noncapital spending. The number of government workers declined for the first time since World War II. (During the Great Society era, government was the fastest growing segment of the labor market.) At the local and state level, slowed population growth, cutbacks in federal aid, the recession, and, most importantly, laws like California's Proposition 13 also reduced the number of employees. Still, government spending remains high. In 1982 spending by the federal, state, and local governments totaled $1,184 billion. That comes to over $5,000 for every man, woman, and child in the country.

In the preferred scenario, balanced federal budgets are not achieved immediately—in fact, not until the late 1980s. Continuing and gradually decreasing deficits are necessary during the early part of the decade. Coupled with tax reductions, gradually decreasing deficits represent a long-range strategy for encouraging work, savings, and investment to improve productivity and economic growth. Three-fourths of the federal budget is considered "uncontrollable," because funds are increased automatically each year by the terms of the original legislation, as the result of inflation and increases in eligible recipients. Interest on the national debt (11 percent of the 1981 budget) and entitlement programs such as Social Security and Medicare are particularly significant parts of the uncontrollable budget. But just as these allocations were legislated, so they can be revised. If we want to control the budget, all we have to do is change the laws.

GOVERNMENT SPENDING TARGETS

We can control government spending by establishing annual state and federal spending targets limited by the rate of economic growth. If the GNP grows by 3.1 percent, then government spending should not exceed this rate. This is a marked departure from the experience of the past 30 years, when government expenditures rose at annual rates substantially higher than GNP growth. Spending targets should gradually slow the growth of both federal and state spending so that, by mid-decade, growth rates advance no faster than those of the chosen measure of economic output. At that time, spending should be reexamined to reduce gradually the target percentages for the second half of the 1980s.

PUBLIC CAPITAL INVESTMENT

The nation's stock of roads, bridges, dams, and public facilities has deteriorated seriously. Over the years, government spending has increasingly been shifted to income maintenance and short-term consumption. Nationwide, public works expenditures accounted for 1.7 percent of GNP in 1980 compared to 4.1 percent of GNP in 1965. The goal of prosperity or even economic recovery is impossible on a foundation of shot railbeds, potholed highways, and leaky water and sewer systems.

The cost of restoration will be high—it is estimated to be over $800 billion in the 1980s. That would be more than all the public works expenditures of all levels of government in the 1970s. In the past large-scale public works projects have been financed with federal pork-barrel funds or by long-term state or local bonds. Federal rules add years to the time needed to complete a project and greatly escalate the costs. At today's high interest rates, the cost of long-term bond financing would be enormous.

In the economic context of the 1980s, it will be advantageous for state and local governments, with the leadership and cooperation of business, to set priorities and develop pay-as-you-go financing plans. State and local tax increases to cover these costs are justified on the basis of keeping the states and localities competitive economically and providing jobs for local people. User fees can cover substantial portions of the maintenance costs. Beyond that, "privatization" should be considered. Private firms would build or restore roads, sewers, and the like with private capital and then lease them back to the local government or charge user fees directly. That approach was followed successfully for a major road between Dallas and Fort Worth. Privatization has several advantages. Business firms are quicker to adopt new technologies, they can get rid of incompetent employees more quickly, and they are generally more efficient. Private firms can also take advantage of accelerated depreciation and investment tax credit incentives.

A combination of some federal funding and the other approaches outlined will be needed to rebuild the nation's infrastructure. The gas tax hike passed by Congress at the end of 1982 will provide an additional $5.5 billion, a step in the right direction. Government expenditures on domestic nondefense programs at local, state, and national levels must be further redirected toward renewal and improvement of public capital facilities. Only 12 percent of total federal nondefense spending for goods and services is now allocated to capital facilities. In the preferred scenario, capital spending is increased to 20 percent by 1990.

REDUCING THE NATIONAL DEBT

The national debt is now in excess of $1 trillion. It has been accumulating for the last four decades, although half of it has been incurred since 1974. At this rate it will reach $2 trillion in less than ten years. Government deficits dampen economic growth, contribute to high interest rates, and weaken national morale. Paying the interest alone costs more than $90 billion a year. It is the third largest item in the federal budget, exceeded only by the cost of social services and national defense. The astronomical size of the debt seems to make it an insurmountable problem. Like other economic threats, however, it can be resolved—first, by deciding to resolve it; second, by choosing a way. Indeed, there are many ways, one of which has been advanced by Charles W. Steadman, chairman of Steadman Security Corporation in Washington, D.C. His proposal is simple and has convincing precedents. Steadman suggests that Congress establish a "public debt repayment trust" to be funded by a 5 percent tax on manufacturers' sales. Sales in 1981 were estimated at $4.2 trillion, which would produce receipts of $210 billion. This money would be applied to paring down the national debt. As the debt is pared down, interest costs would decline and the entire debt could be liquidated. Steadman believes that reducing the service costs alone can provide a basis for lowering taxes, provide an actual federal surplus, and work to reduce interest rates. More importantly, such a commitment would inspire confidence in business investment, greatly stimulating the economy.

This proposal is modeled after the Federal Highway Trust Fund, which was established by Congress in 1965 to fund the development of the interstate highway system, one of the most successful federal programs ever instituted. It was successful precisely because there was no deviation from purpose and no diversion of funds.

Increasing taxes is of course only one approach to reducing federal deficits. Of equal importance are efforts to reduce federal spending, especially the enormous military budget.

INDIVIDUAL RESPONSIBILITY VERSUS GOVERNMENT REGULATION

James Madison warned, "It will be of little avail to the people that laws are made by men of their own choosing, if the laws are so voluminous that they cannot be read, or so incoherent that they cannot be understood, or undergo such change that no man who knows what the law is today can guess what it will be tomorrow." Unfortunately, Madison's warning seems to apply to government regulation in this country today. Excessive, inefficient business regulations add to the cost of producing goods and services, reduce investment and thus productivity growth, increase uncertainty in the business environment, stifle competition, discourage innovation, and overload the nation's legal and administrative systems.

Substantial progress has been made toward deregulation in recent years, but much remains to be done. Lowering the federal minimum wage for the young, for example, will open up entry level job markets for thousands of youths, thus restoring a step on the economic ladder for young or poorly trained persons, particularly among minorities. At the present high minimum wage, poorly trained people cost prospective employers more than the employers are willing to spend. But at lower minimum wages, employers would have greater incentives to offer on-the-job training. Being unable to get a job at all makes it impossible for a worker's skills to improve and thereby condemns the person to a vicious cycle.

Senator Patrick Moynihan of New York noted a decade ago that welfare payments had actually become competitive with employment. Because working persons could earn little more than their welfare check, and sometimes even less because of taxation, an actual economic incentive existed for staying on welfare rather than seeking work. Obviously, policies like these must be changed if productivity is to improve.

All living subsidy payments that emphasize the "dole" rather than human recovery, regeneration, and reclamation must be rethought and revamped—including Social Security and public pensions.

Until recently, the government approach to regulation has been direct rule making rather than positive incentives that would promote the best solution at the lowest cost. Direct rule making removes the ability to deal flexibly with a diverse and changing economy. Rule making by the Environmental Protection Agency (EPA) provides an example. Environmental protection rules that require the most advanced technology paradoxically work to discourage that same technology; companies often are forced to resort to makeshift technology because EPA deadlines allow insufficient time for fundamental engineering and retooling. The current rule-making approach to regulation is cumbersome, corruptible, and arbitrary.

We have come to accept a government role in many areas that actually may be better handled by private initiative and economic incentives. We think of environmental protection as solely the responsibility of government, for example, although there is considerable evidence that the initiative of private individuals working through voluntary organizations can realize substantial environmental goals. One example is Ducks Unlimited, an association of sportsmen, hunters, conservationists, and bird watchers interested in the welfare of water fowl. Since its founding after World War II, the nearly 400,000 members of this organization have raised over $133 million to preserve over 2.9 million acres of wildlife habitat in Canadian provinces and in the northwest United States. Seventy percent of the continent's water fowl nest in these areas each year. Without Ducks Unlimited, entire species of water fowl would probably have become extinct.

Multiply the initiative and positive results of Ducks Unlimited by a thousand other interests, and it is obvious that intelligent and purposeful private responsibility can be effective in managing and preserving the environment—as well as in accomplishing many other things now thought to be the sole preserve of government.

ENERGY: RANGE OF OPTIONS

The Arab oil embargo of 1973 and the Iranian cutoff of 1979 clearly demonstrated the consequences—both economic and in terms of resource availability—of dependence on foreign energy sources. Thus it is essential that national policy choices move toward greater energy self-sufficiency.

The preferred scenario requires maintaining production of domestic gas and oil at the 1978 level of 39 quads per year through 2000. But we also must utilize alternative sources. If oil imports come down to 30 percent of total oil consumption as a consequence, we still will have an adequate energy supply for a steady 3 percent growth in GNP. If the public can accomplish this goal, by 2000 we will need imports only for 6 percent of total energy use. But to maintain 1978 levels of oil, we will have to find and develop new deposits, a task harder than it sounds. There is a difference between oil resources and oil reserves. Oil resources are those deposits with some potential for recovery. Oil reserves are those that can be recovered economically with current technology at prevailing prices.

The United States Geological Survey estimates that the country has 27 billion barrels of reserves. There are perhaps 80 billion barrels of resources. The United States has been using reserves faster than it develops new ones, which is why companies have begun exploring the Outer Continental Shelf. There may be as much as 38 billion barrels on the shelf, or there may be as little as 12 billion barrels.

New recovery techniques can literally squeeze oil out of stone. Heat, chemicals, waterflooding, and steam injection thin out oil in rock formations and push it toward existing wells, although these processes are more expensive than conventional drilling. More often than not, these resources exist in inaccessible places, which adds to the expense of extracting them.

Accelerated leasing of federal lands—on- and offshore—is essential to our energy independence. The federal government owns one-third of the land in the United States and all of the Outer Continental Shelf. Federal agencies control 62 percent of Alaska's area, 48 percent of Wyoming's, 47 percent of California's, 37 percent of Colorado's, and 33 percent of New Mexico's. The government, charged with protecting the wilderness and the environment, does not hand out passports to oil drillers readily. Only 4 percent of submerged federal lands have been leased and only 13 percent of onshore lands, but not simply because government is trying to preserve the view. Drilling releases harmful dust and gas, affects underground water supplies, and makes noise that can be almost maddening.

Considering the variables—geology, price, technology, and regulations—we could shrink production by 19 percent in the next 20 years or expand it by 12 percent. It all depends on the choices we make.

Another option is natural gas, an energy mainstay of the economy. First, it burns cleanly. Second, almost all of what we use we produce domestically, about 20 thousand cubic feet a year. We have enough to last only another 40 years at present consumption levels. Gas producers and consumers, however, have been locked in a crucial debate: Should the price of gas be set on the cost of production or on its value in the marketplace? The nation only recently decided on the latter. Gas producers thus have incentives that will boost production when prices are deregulated in 1985.

Coal, with a reserve of 437 billion tons, is our most abundant energy resource. There is no danger of these reserves running out for 300 years. But coal also poses a serious question: Can we burn it safely without damaging our health and environment? Coal releases proportionately more carbon dioxide than oil or gas, and synthetic liquid fuels made from coal release even more. "Scrubbers" and "precipitators" clean sulfur dioxide and all but the smallest particulates released by burning coal. Inserting ammonia into combustion gases cleans out nitrogen oxides. Fluidized bed combustion, a new technology that burns coal in a turbulent "bed" of air with limestone injected to capture sulfur oxides, turns these gases into harmless solids. It is virtually 100 percent effective.

But these technologies are savagely expensive. In 1978 the utility industry spent $4 billion on scrubbers alone. The desirability of coal, then, is a function of having it in great abundance.

Synthetics are not a near-term solution either. True, there is more oil in the United States' shale deposits than in the petroleum reserves of all the OPEC nations combined. But the rock has to be mined, brought to the surface, crushed into fragments from 0.25 to 3 inches, and then heated in a free-standing chimneylike vessel, called a retort. Some developers have tried *in situ* retorting. The earth itself becomes the chimney, and shale rubble is heated underground. Even with this advanced method, synthetic fuels cost more than oil or gas, and the extraction is perilous.

The sun gives us the equivalent of 500,000 billion barrels of oil every day. But collecting this energy, concentrating it, and converting it into other energy forms makes solar energy expensive. Solar heating systems that work can be incorporated into commercial buildings and homes as long as it is not cloudy and no object, such as a tall building, blocks the sun.

One obvious and immediate answer to energy supply problems is nuclear-generated power. Despite public fear of nuclear reactors, nuclear power is already here. It has proved itself an efficient source of energy. It needs no refinements to make it practical, although (as with any technology) it will undergo continual refinements to make it cheaper and to reduce further the already minimal risks.

The cost of enriched uranium fuel is almost negligible over the operating life of a nuclear plant. By contrast, fuel and the burning of it are the largest costs in using other energy sources. Once a nuclear system goes onto operation, there is much less uncertainty about the costs of operation. Nuclear power tempers the competition for scarce fossil fuels, especially from the Middle East, where political upheavals can disrupt supplies at any time.

In March 1979 one of the reactors generating power at the Three Mile Island plant near Harrisburg, Pennsylvania suffered damages in the reactor core, although the integrity of the containment system was not impaired. Only negligible amounts of radiation escaped, exposing the surrounding environment to no more than what are considered normal radiation levels in Denver, Albuquerque, or other high altitude cities.

Public concern and media sensationalism made this accident a near catastrophe. Congress conducted an exhaustive review of nuclear licensing. The electric utility industry expanded training of operating personnel, and nuclear suppliers promised a more comprehensive and comprehensible design of instrumentation. The investigations, however, consumed considerable time and the result was a long delay during which no licenses for other reactors were granted.

What was feared did not happen and, factually, could not happen. But the industry built on the experience to strengthen its plants and operating procedures. On this new foundation, the United States must make a stronger national commitment to nuclear energy, with the federal government regulating the transportation of nuclear materials, their reprocessing and waste disposal.

France, England, West Germany, Japan, and the Soviet Union have all made major commitments to increasing their nuclear-generating capacity. Statistics from Electricité de France price a nuclear kilowatt-hour at 2.06 mills in 1980, down from 2.1 mills in 1979 and 3.5 mills in 1972. France now has 22 nuclear units. Officials promise to generate 70 percent of the country's power from nuclear stations in 1990, reducing the cost of power by half that in neighboring European countries. The combined factors of nuclear's economic and environmental advantages and its excellent safety record along with the likelihood of a rebound in the price of oil argue for continued commitment to the use and expansion of nuclear power.

RESOLVING THE THREAT OF NUCLEAR WAR

The resolution of economic and energy threats to survival will ease the pressures now building toward the threat of nuclear war.

In addition to ideological fixations of the superpowers, the arms race is being fueled by competition and conflict over scarce international energy supplies. As the information economy expands, U.S. energy demand in relation to GNP will drop. The economic and energy choices that this book recommends will increase productivity, control inflation, and make the United States self-sufficient in energy over time. All of these developments should defuse the need for a defense buildup.

Other social and economic forces are also working toward a resolution of the threat posed by nuclear arms. The economic cost of an expanded nuclear war machine grows increasingly beyond the capacities of the U.S. and Soviet economies to support. When added to the requirements of maintaining conventional military preparedness, the costs of an accelerated program of nuclear armaments become unbearable. In the United States there is a direct chain from rapidly growing military expenditures to federal budget deficits to continuing high interest rates to a generation that cannot afford owning its own homes. Soviet arms spending has greatly weakened the domestic economy of that nation: they are dependent on the United States for food, trade fully one-quarter of their GNP in the black market, and sell huge quantities of gold to cover trade imbalances.

Reducing military spending is the largest obstacle to achieving the preferred economic scenario. As in all other areas, this is a matter of economic and social choices. Millions of men and women are diverted from productive civilian pursuits, millions of barrels of oil are consumed without adding to useful capital or consumer goods and services, and thousands of square miles of land are removed from production. The real cost of allocating all of these productive resources to war preparations is that they are not available for other purposes. The brain drain alone is enormous.

In a 1982 study Employment Research Associates of Lansing, Michigan, found that increased military spending adds to unemployment by draining away funds that, if spent elsewhere, would generate more jobs. They reported that, compared to 14,000 jobs in guided missiles and ordinance, $1 billion would generate 65,000 jobs in retail trade, 62,000 jobs in education, 48,000 jobs in hospitals,

30,000 jobs in newspapers, 28,000 jobs in apparel manufacturing, or 16,000 jobs in metal fabrication.*

The New York-based Council on Economic Priorities studied the economies of Western European countries, Japan, and the United States and concluded that those countries with smaller military budgets enjoy faster economic growth and bigger increases in investment and productivity. Military spending can be financed only at the cost of private investment or by increasing the money supply, both of which promote higher interest rates and inflation.

Paul Volcker, chairman of the Federal Reserve Board, which governs the nation's money supply and monetary policy, was asked in a Congressional hearing about the inflationary effect of defense spending. He responded, "The point is often made, Senator, that defense spending, by its nature, producing goods that are put on the shelf, so far as the economy is concerned—and they may be terribly important in terms of the national interest but they don't provide satisfaction for consumer wants—can have a more inflationary impact, I suppose, than even transfer payments." "I do think there are problems from the inflation standpoint in rapid increases in defense spending."†

The economic drag of military spending hits small business especially hard. A position paper issued in September 1982 by the International Business Network, a group devoted to supporting small businesses, contains these statements: "the nation's current economic stagnation is directly related to the ever-escalating arms race." "According to official Department of Defense figures, only one dollar in five goes to small business [firms of 500 or fewer employees]. Yet, study after study has shown that small companies are the most innovative, and produce goods at the most competitive prices." "A study by James Capra, an economic analyst for the Federal Reserve Bank of New York, reveals that the cost of defense items is rising rapidly. 'If you compare purchase plans and expenditures on a year-by-year basis, you find we are spending a lot more and buying a lot less. Unit prices are going way up.' Capra told the

---

*Employment Research Associates, *The Empty Pork Barrel* (Lansing, Mich.: ERA, 1982).
†Volcker testimony before Senate Banking Committee, February 25, 1981.

International Business Network." "America is undergoing a severe economic crisis, one that can only be ended by bringing the federal budget into balance reducing the current disastrously high interest rates inflicted on small business."*

Small business is the primary source of new employment in the United States; yet small business receives the most adverse impact from the government's largest single source of spending—the defense budget.

Considering the scale and redundancy of the nuclear destructive capability already at hand, engaging in an arms race to build more cannot be considered anything other than insane. It is like the man who was obsessed with hot dogs and could not see why he should be sent to see a psychiatrist just because he kept all the closets in his house full of hot dogs. The house full of hot dogs is sober sanity compared to the accumulation of more nuclear weapons.

People on both sides of the cold war are coming to realize that change in arms spending will come only from a groundswell of public opinion. Polls in the United States reveal strong support for controlling arms and for negotiating agreements with the Soviet Union. Worker unrest in Soviet bloc countries reveals a growing intolerance of food shortages resulting from the continued diversion of resources to military purposes.

Resolving the threat of nuclear arms is a matter of moral as well as practical economic choices on the part of individuals. Admiral Stansfield Turner, who served as director of the CIA during the Carter Administration and who serves now as an international relations consultant, has addressed this point directly:

> The American public needs to inform itself on this basic issue and then let its feeling be heard. This does not require an understanding of complex technical issues. The issue has less to do with weapons characteristics than it does with how we believe world leaders will react in time of tension and how comfortable or uncomfortable we feel as a nation with our state of nuclear preparedness. The informed citizen can judge those questions as well or better than the military

---

*International Business Network, "Record Defense Budgets Harmful to Small Business: Expert Urges Reagan to Consider New Russian Offer," *Position Paper*, Santa Monica, Calif., September 16, 1982, pp. 5-6.

expert, who is immersed in his megatonnage and inclined to assess the issue by analyzing technology rather than human nature.*

The threat of nuclear weapons cannot be resolved by technical solutions. Building a defensive antiballistic missile system would not add to deterrence but merely be another step in the race to gain strategic advantage. The only deterrence is knowledge and the will to use it. We must change the way we think about war and how to relate with one another.

In his book *The Fate of the Earth*, Jonathan Schell traces the purpose and logic of war as an extension of politics. Before the advent of nuclear weapons, the function of war was to decide issues of territory, resources, people, or ideas. Schell reasons conclusively that any war involving the major powers would ultimately become nuclear war and that nuclear war would destroy all objects of gain—including human life. Thus humanity has moved beyond the utility of war. War no longer serves a useful purpose.† When that reality sinks in, the economic and political dimensions pale, and the nuclear arms issue can be seen as the most profound religious issue of this or any time. The only resolution of the problem will be through a shift in attitude among people, along with the vigorous pursuit of agreements on arms reduction control.

---

*Stansfield Turner, "Is the U.S. Pinning False Hopes on the MX System?" *Los Angeles Times*, September 20, 1981, pt. 5, p. 3.

†Jonathan Schell, *The Fate of the Earth* (New York: Alfred A. Knopf, 1982), chapt. 3.

5
Models for a Preferred Path to Prosperity

In a time of major change and great uncertainty, people need guides–individuals who serve as models of successful adjustments and transitions. As models for a preferred path to prosperity, these individuals represent a different kind of leadership than the national heroes we customarily invoke. U.S. history is filled with examples of men and women whose names are unknown to a public that has benefited from their talent and energy. These individuals have not sought attention but instead have dedicated themselves to service. Their contributions, incremental rather than revolutionary, have added to the record of U.S. achievements in the last half century and to a national fiber that has sustained us through an unprecedented series of shocks and crises.

Theirs is a highly productive brand of leadership, not linked to any specific station in life. A precise characterization of their style is impossible, but there are some common threads: an underlying optimism or faith in a positive future, a long-term view and commitment to a broad goal, a willingness to take risks (or, conversely, a recognition that security is an illusion), and the ability to work cooperatively in service to the community.

These common themes surface repeatedly in the following ten profiles. While many people drain their energies resisting change, these people simply respond to new needs. Our models are drawn from many different fields: business, labor, government, nonprofit volunteer organizations, education, journalism, agriculture, and religion. Business heads the list because that sector, more than any other, is oriented to risk taking, uncertainty, and change. Within the business sector, two industries stand out as having undergone truly revolutionary changes in the last decade: electric utilities and personal computers. The first model illustrates change and adaptation in the context of a large business organization. This model is presented in the profiles of two men who lived through the transformation of one electric utility company and left their personal marks on it. The second model presents the opposite end of the spectrum of U.S. industry, the small business entrepreneur. Of equal importance are the contributions of other individuals to their respective fields.

JACK HORTON

Jack K. Horton was president and later chairman and chief executive officer of the Southern California Edison Company (SCE) for some 20 years before he retired in 1980. He now serves as a director and chairman of the executive committee of the board and as a consultant to the company. The word "retired" is not appropriate for Horton's full schedule of assignments, meetings, and travel.

On one of the paneled walls of Horton's office, hanging among proclamations recognizing his public service over the years, is a framed needlepoint from his wife, which reads, "Do not wish to be anything but what you are, and try to be that perfectly," a simple adage that characterizes the man. He is open and unassuming.

Horton's description of the revolutionary changes through which he led the Southern California Edison Company is characteristically understated: "Utilities live in the future. They have to see a decade ahead. It takes years to build a plant to produce electric energy. We have to anticipate where the need will be, where people will settle. Then we have to find the most advantageous location to service this impending need. There is a long line of permits and approvals before we construct a power plant and start stringing the wires."

"When I came in as president in 1959, load growth was increasing at 8 to 9 percent per year. If you wanted to build a power plant, you decided what was the most efficient plant and location and you went and built it; nobody opposed it. It was all based on economics and what's best for the consumer. At that time we competed with the gas company for the energy market. We had a marketing department to promote sales of electricity and an area development department which worked to get industry to locate in our service territory. Growth and system expansion were a way of life in the electric utility business.

"The whole situation changed in the late 1960s and early 1970s. There was the rise of environmental concerns and social protests in general. Utility companies were viewed as an adversary instead of a public servant. The question of growth and development became an issue, and we had to rethink our ways of doing business. The environmentalists changed our thinking, but the real revolution came with the rise in oil prices. Nobody anticipated that: not I, not foreign affairs experts. Nobody thought oil would go from $2 a barrel to $40."

Utility companies consume vast quantities of oil. Imagine one of the towering chimneys of a generating plant. At its circular base are four furnaces: east, west, north, and south. These furnaces are 20 feet high by 6 feet wide and 6 feet deep. They sometimes burn oil 24 hours a day to heat the water in the labyrinth of pipes for producing the steam that spins the turbines. Southern California Edison Company is one of the largest oil users in the country.

"Expensive oil," said Horton, "set in motion a chain of events that transformed the economics of electric utility operations. Most obvious to the public was the dramatic increase in rates. For example, the desert town of Palm Springs uses extraordinary amounts of electricity in the summer. The older houses were built for winter occupancy only, but now people live in them year-round. Because they are not adequately insulated in many cases, the cost of air-conditioning is high. Palm Springs has protest groups that appear before regulatory bodies at every opportunity. It's a terrible problem, not just for Palm Springs but for all electricity users. The company can't force oil prices down, but we can't throw up our hands in despair either. We have had to respond to the change. When prices started up in 1974, I told our planning people that we were underestimating the effect on electricity use. Load growth at 6 percent or 7 percent was a pattern of the past. Our projected load growth now for the next 10 years is in the range of 2 percent per year, and that represents 78,000 new customers annually.

"Southern California Edison had spent many years selling its product; now we unsell it. We work very hard at convincing our customers to use less. When the oil embargo interrupted our fuel supplies, we had to ask our customers to conserve electricity out of patriotism, which they did. When the price of oil shot up, we asked people to conserve electricity out of self-interest, which they still are doing. We converted our marketing department into a conservation department. We'll send experts out to your home to do energy audits and recommend ways to conserve power. We disbanded the Area Development Department. Industries are now investing capital to conserve energy because energy is so expensive.

"With inflation and high interest rates, I am not sure that any company in our industry could have financed a program aimed at increasing load growth. It would be disastrous to invest in new plants and new transmission lines that are not desperately needed."

To make the Edison company responsive to the rapidly changing business environment, Horton changed its internal organization and processes dramatically. He restructured the organization to consolidate customer service functions and to push responsibility down to the local level; he instituted weekly "officers' council meetings" to improve communication; he launched a long-range strategic planning process requiring managers to assess carefully the constantly changing operating environment. He built a major research and development capability and says with pride, "We spend more on research and development than any utility in the country. I always insisted to our vice-presidents that when someone presents a proposal you think is crazy, you better take a long and careful look at it. It is important to find out whether he's crazy or you're crazy."

When the federal government was going to build the Pacific Intertie—a high-technology transmission line—to bring low-cost power from the state of Washington to Southern California, Horton in his characteristic manner worked in a mode of cooperation and compromise to assure the participation of private companies.

Horton talks about the willingness to experiment: "I've learned the importance of creating an atmosphere of openness in which the officers and department heads are free to communicate without fear of harassment if they recommend something that their boss doesn't like."

In 1975 SCE received an award for excellence from *Electric Light and Power* magazine, which characterized the company as "an agile giant." In Jack Horton we see flexibility and a willingness to change, combined with an ethic of service and stewardship. This ethic emerged early in his life. He was born in rural Nebraska in 1916, and his father died in the influenza epidemic when Jack was two. He was raised by his grandparents while his mother worked. His grandmother pushed him academically so that he could skip some grades in school. "I've had mixed feelings about that all my life," Horton says. "I was a couple of years younger than my classmates through high school and college, which was interesting, but I just wasn't big enough. I did all my emotional growing after my freshman year at Stanford."

Jack chose Stanford University in California, following his brother, primarily because he could work his way through college. After graduating in 1963, in the heart of the Great Depression, his major in economics landed him a job in the mailroom of the Shell Oil Company in San Francisco at $100 a month, an irony that never fails to amuse the story teller. "About that same time I was married to Betty Lou Magee, and with her encouragement I went to law school at night." In five years Horton passed the bar exam and became the credit manager in the very office where he had started delivering mail. He decided to try out being a lawyer and was going to build a law practice in a smaller city, but the war changed his plans. He joined Standard Oil Company of California in San Francisco, expecting to be drafted soon. He applied for a commission with naval intelligence, but the Navy turned him down because of his poor eyesight.

"It turned out to be lucky for me because the war drained off great numbers of personnel at Standard Oil, including lawyers. I was immediately involved in a multimillion dollar suit for the company over the Elk Hills Oil Field, a naval petroleum reserve. I worked with the senior vice-president and the president in developing legislation which allowed Elk Hills to supply oil.

"After that, Standard Oil asked me to go over to one of its subsidiaries in San Francisco, a holding company which owned Coast Counties Gas and Electric Company. Well, I thought I'd rather be a big frog in a small puddle than a specialist with a large company. As secretary and legal counsel for Coast Counties, I got into everything. I wrote the first collective bargaining agreement when the union was established. I did the work with the Securities and Exchange Commission on financing, and as secretary I handled the board meetings.

I tried a case before the Public Utilities Commission for an increase in natural gas rates and won it by initiating compromises."

The mode of cooperation and flexibility paid off; Horton was made president of Coast Counties when he was 35 years old. When the company was sold to Pacific Gas and Electric Company, he decided to stay with the new owners. "The people at Coast Counties were uneasy about merging into the Goliath and by staying I helped them find their proper place. By staying I also thought I would be able to live in California. With Standard Oil, I could get transferred anywhere in the world."

But Horton was in for a surprise—within the year, PG&E sent him to Alberta, Canada, a crucial assignment in his career. The company wanted to augment its natural gas supplies by piping gas from Alberta, but the project was being opposed by both U.S. and Canadian interests. "The West Coast Transmission Company, a Canadian pipeline, fought against us, and so did the El Paso Natural Gas Company. PG&E was the captive customer of the only existing pipleine owned by El Paso Natural Gas and needed another source. Winning the right to sink the pipeline was a delicate operation. In the 1950s Canadians resented American investment that exploited their resources. Many Canadians, however, knew that their economy couldn't thrive without U.S. dollars. Nevertheless, Canadians were often fiercely nationalistic and deeply despised Americans who threw their weight around."

When all the arrangements were made, the proposed pipeline was to cross a small corner of British Columbia. The day Horton went to put his case before the governor of the province, someone leaked the news of the pipeline's path to the papers. When Horton saw the premier in his office in Victoria, the man said, "Don't bother to sit down, Mr. Horton. I know why you're here. Nobody's going to build a pipeline across British Columbia to take Alberta gas to California." "Mr. Premier," said Horton, "I'd hoped you would look at this project as a Canadian." "I'll remind you," said the premier, "that my oath of allegiance is to the province, not to the Crown."

Horton found out later that the premier's oath indeed was to the Crown—the pipeline was built across British Columbia. Horton succeeded because he recruited Canadian partners who knew the law. He also cooperated with the competition by giving West Coast Transmission a share of the ownership in the segment of the line that passed through British Columbia. Most importantly, he offered the sale of common stock to Canadians before offering it on U.S. exchanges.

In 1958, when Horton was getting ready to come back to PG&E in San Francisco, Harold Quinton, the head of Southern California Edison Company, called him to Los Angeles and asked him to be executive vice-president of the utility. Horton responded that he was satisfied where he was, but if Quinton wanted to move up as chairman of the board and bring Horton in as president, that was an offer he would consider. "It was something I threw out," said Horton, "like quoting an impossible price for a house. But to my surprise Quinton took the matter up with his executive committee that morning and before noon I had a new job. I asked that the effective date of my election be delayed three months so I could finish my assignment in Canada."

Horton says, "My rule has been to stand firm on matters of principle and be flexible on matters of taste. To give an example from family life, when we moved to Los Angeles I felt it was important for us to join a church. It turned out that our daughter Sally, who was in third grade, wanted us to go to a church in Beverely Hills, which her teacher attended. This was not as convenient as other churches nearby, but that was a matter of taste; why argue about something like that when the important thing was that the family be in a church and go regularly, and the kids go to Sunday school."

Horton's style of flexibility and cooperation added greatly to his personal success and that of SCE as an institution.

BILL GOULD

When Jack Horton retired as chairman and chief executive officer of Southern California Edison in July 1980, he was succeeded by William R. Gould, who had served as president.

Bill Gould started work at the Southern California Edison Company in 1948 as an engineer. For more than ten years, as he worked his way up in the organization, the operating climate was quite stable, marked by steady growth and continual plant construction. As an engineer oriented to building, it would have been easy for Gould to have resisted change when it came. But in his soul Bill Gould is an innovator, a positive spirit willing to let go of old ways and put faith in the new.

It is common among leaders to have surmounted adversity in their early lives, and this was the case with Bill Gould. He was born in 1919, a sickly child, frail and skinny, who developed a pronounced stutter. His father was a railroad engineer, who was frequently away from the small adobe house in Provo, Utah, but he often took Bill along on his runs. "When I was 16 years old," Bill says, "I threw coal with a scoop shovel into a steam locomotive. Today, I am a trustee of a corporation which produces the technology supporting the space shuttle. Quite a journey."

This early experience with railroads interested Bill in machinery and led to his choice of profession. He decided to become a mechanical engineer, work requiring skills that did not put a premium on the ability to speak. Gould does not stutter now; in fact, his delivery is virtually professional. While he was a student at the University of Utah, he married Erlyn Johnson, who went to great lengths to help him overcome his impediment. "She was one of the turning points in my life," said Gould. "I won her and learned to speak clearly, which is like being released from a prison into heaven."

Gould grew to maturity in the late 1930s. He was 19 when Hitler invaded Poland. "I was aware of the frightful turbulence in the world and also aware of a burgeoning technology which would change my life as much as Hitler did." He joined the Reserve Officer Training Corps at Utah, "a horse-drawn artillery outfit. We have also trained as mounted cavalry. I knew I was in an arcane branch of warfare and tried to transfer, but a colonel sternly admonished me that this war is going to be decided on horseback. I was determined to resign my commission and accept another in the navy as an ensign." This early decision to let go of something familiar and move to something unknown had far-reaching effects in Gould's life.

"The navy gave me a series of assignments absolutely consonant with my professional training. In my first two years of service, I got ten years of experience. I built submarines and submarine tenders, repaired British cruisers which had been shot to pieces, helped build the battleship South Dakota in the Philadelphia Navy Yard, served as the sea trials officer at San Pedro—took new ships on their shakedown cruises, certified the crews, and learned everything about steam propulsion plants. I relished my work so much that when the war ended I decided to make the navy my career. But after two years in Boston, the pace slowed and the spirit was gone; so I gave up my commission to enter civilian life. Shortly after that, Southern California Edison Company offered me a job.

"At that time the company was embarking on two major projects: one was a change in frequency from 50 to 60 cycles, and the other was a huge growth in generating capacity. When I started, my sights were set on a good engineering job; I had no thoughts about the executive suite. I always focused on the task immediately in front of me. All I wanted to do was make ten yards so I could get a new set of downs. Then I would decide where I would go from there.

"In 1947 a utility company was considered a pillar of the industrial community; nothing else was as solid. Half the world traded on utility company credit. One out of every ten dollars invested in capital goods was invested in the electric utility industry. SCE was one of the largest utilities, and we were growing at a rate of 9 percent per year compounded. There was no adverse reaction to putting plants in neighborhoods and on sea coasts. In the two decades after the war, we were the commercial and industrial heroes.

"There were several attempts during that time to lure me away from Edison. Manufacturing companies offered more compensation, but I turned them down. I always felt that I wanted to be working on multidisciplinary engineering projects rather than gadgets. With Edison I was engaged in a product essential to the life support system of our society."

"In my early years I was directly responsible for the operation of the system. We fought against the elements—fires and floods—endangering an electric system covering 50,000 square miles with much of its facilities overhead and aboveground, a system which enters the backyard of every residence in the southern part of the state. There were times when the ability to keep machines on line was an act of will rather than engineering skill. One night, we had the entire hillside above Malibu in flames with most of our distribution and transmission facilities burned or threatened. I had to coax men down from the poles, men who had worked 36 and more hours, force them to get some rest. I had to restrain men from running into hazardous locations. These were the same men we argued with over labor contracts, but when the system and its integrity were at stake, they worked hard and took perilous chances."

Gould was born a Mormon and retains a deep and abiding commitment to the church. He is president of the Long Beach East

Stake, which encompasses 11 congregations and whose bishops report to him in the performance of their duties. Judging from his record of past posts and positions in different organizations, he has always gravitated toward leadership, taking its burdens much to heart. Referring to his role for many years as a bishop in the Church of Latter Day Saints, he says, "The bishop serves on the cutting edge of the social, spiritual, temporal, and personal lives of the people in the congregation. He agonizes with, he counsels with, he laughs with, he cries with the people. He is in their lives in a very intimate and meaningful way. He serves completely without compensation. Frequently he laughs and says he pays for the privilege of serving. Nevertheless, it is a very rewarding thing. I have often been reminded of the words of Rudyard Kipling, who said: 'I have eaten your bread and salt. I have drunk your water and wine. The deaths ye died I have watched beside, and the lives ye led were mine. Was there aught that I did not share in vigil, toil or ease. One joy or woe that I did not know, dear hearts across the seas.'* This is the way I feel about that kind of service, one of the most rewarding and fulfilling experiences I have ever had."

Gould views the responsibilities of corporate leadership much as he does his church service: "I sometimes stand at the window at the close of a business day and watch the people leaving the building. I'm always struck that each one is a person who has hopes and dreams and all of the spectrum of feelings that I have. They go to their homes, most of them to families where they hope to have the warmth and the security that a home provides. I've always been impressed with the responsibility I have to maintain the corporation as a viable entity wherein those hopes and dreams can be realized."

Gould's sensitivity to the full effects of his decisions on people's lives does not lessen his decisiveness. Of his management and decision-making style, he says, "I have always guided by two strategies. There were always those who were smarter than I was, and I would have to compensate for their facility by hard work and organization. And I always felt that each event should follow its predecessor as rapidly as possible. Thus you move quickly from contemplating the problem

---

*Rudyard Kipling, prelude to "Departmental Duties," *Rudyard Kipling Verse: The Definitive Edition*, 1885.

to solving it. I therefore devoted singular energies to defining the problem. I saved a great deal of time often by realizing there were no options or alternatives. My friend Jack Horton always said, 'if you have no alternative, you have no problem.' I have never worried about the 70-yard touchdown run. I want to make 10 yards and get a new set of downs."

In October 1980, three months after taking the reins as chief executive officer of SCE, Bill Gould announced a landmark decision with enormous consequences for the organization as well as society at large. The company set a goal of producing 30 percent of the new energy needed for its customers by 1990 using renewable and alternative energy sources, including hydroelectric, wind, solar (both thermal and photovoltaic), fuel cells, geothermal, and cogeneration. This was an industry first, and the announcement was accompanied by widespread acclaim by the news media and the public. But Gould insists it was hardly a new idea. "Actually, the decision had its genesis quite a number of years before, even in the days when we were actively building large steam-generating stations and heavy transmission systems. During those years, there were thoughts forming in my mind that later came in focus when we were facing this renewable and alternate energy question. I was impressed with the fact that there was a finite limit to fuel sources. There was also a finite limit to the air, water, and land resources required to build a heavy integrated electric system. We have not approached the limits, but the general public grew to have little patience and less tolerance as we consumed these resources. The air quality management districts are now using the principle of tradeoffs when they approve new projects. For each new increment of an air-consuming facility to come into service, for each new burden placed on the airshed by combustion, an existing one must disappear. This is an indication that the limits are being approached on that particular resource. Back in the 1960s, I wrote an article for the *General Electric Forum* in which I expressed these kinds of concerns."

Gould's article reveals a deep feeling for the relationship between humanity and the environment. In 1967 he wrote, "Among the elementary environmental factors identified by the ancient Greeks were earth, air, and water. It is around these elements of our ecology that the energy-producing industry faces its greatest challenges." In the same article Gould sets forth the ethic of service coupled with a belief in cooperation as the way to deal with problems. "Because governmental agencies and the utilities alike are

86 / PATHWAYS TO PROSPERITY

servants of the same ultimate 'customers,' the general public, we must cooperate to the best ultimate interest of that public. In my opinion this demands a recognition by each of the responsible roles of the other. It demands full and honest communication of intent and objective, and a thorough discussion of the social problems with which we are mutually concerned, together with a thorough evaluation of alternate solutions to them."

Sitting in his office in 1982, Gould recalled discussions in the early 1970s with Edison's new research and development group about the need to develop "a technology that would produce small increments of generating capacity that could be moved around the system without the necessity to build large transmission lines."

To the public and much of the electric utility industry, the decision to move to renewable and alternative energy sources was a major change in direction. To Bill Gould it was part of an evolutionary process of gaining ten yards and a new first down. It was the natural outcome of a strategy of cooperating with a changing environment.

A major change of course by a large organization is not accomplished by a single announcement from the person at the top. To assure implementation of the decision, Gould appointed a committee of officers and managers that came to be known informally as the "make-it-happen" committee. As this name implies, the new goal had an energizing effect on employees throughout the organization. When early success was achieved in the areas of hydroelectric power and cogeneration, the overall goal was increased accordingly. Focus on the goal generated an entrepreneurial spirit and loosened up traditional operating modes. For example, the company had always sought to own and operate its own generating facilities. Now is was entering into joint ventures and partnerships in which outside investors put up the capital and shared the risks. The attitude of openness and flexibility at the top permeated the organization, bringing an emphasis on innovation to all levels of SCE.

The response to the decision was overwhelmingly positive. After an initial rush of favorable comments from the press, public officials, and public interest speakers, SCE received a series of prestigious awards from environmental and conservation organizations. The company's stock prices and bond ratings showed new strength. Bill

Gould was named an outstanding chief executive officer. In early 1983, after two years of experience with the project, the company announced it was slightly ahead of schedule in meeting its decade of the 1980s commitment.

With regard to the factors that led to the decision to pursue alternative and renewable energy sources, Gould says, "The long lead times imposed on major projects and regulatory pressure began to take their toll, but the economic changes caused by rising oil prices and high interest rates were most influential. Also, the investment we had made earlier in research and development in the search for alternatives had started to pay off in terms of technological feasibility. Environmental concerns played a part in the decision, but having the technology within reach, plus the economic considerations, was paramount. There are utilities that have rattled the saber when they met opposition. They insisted somewhat heatedly that if they could not expand their system, they would not be able to serve the public. We decided not to do that. We made a conscious decision that we would not abandon our commitment to serve the public, that we would discharge our responsibility to the public trust, that somehow we would find a way to serve. It was with this in mind that we made our announcement about alternative resources. We haven't been disappointed in our choice. What we really gave up was comfort, and I have given up comfort many times in the past."

Looking at the country as a whole, Gould says, "There are certain immutable laws of economics. First, if you're going to produce a major change, you have to take the wealth from current economic production. You must commit existing wealth for future development. Unfortunately, this is not being done today in our society. Second, if you use a larger increment of present wealth to build a project than is used by another country, you're going to run second. This is what America has been doing. Japan and West Germany do not have our institutionalized approval procedures so they don't have to commit as much of their present wealth to get things done. We read that productivity of Japan and West Germany is higher than the United States. This is one of the reasons why."

Under the leadership of Bill Gould and Jack Horton, the Southern California Edison Company is a model of productive investment and successful adaptation to a changing environment.

JIM ROSEBORO

As the owner of a small business, Dr. James A. Roseboro operates on a very different scale than the leaders of the Southern California Edison Company. Being the entrepreneur of a small business is a personal act of risk taking and of faith in the future.

Jim Roseboro is not only a medical physicist with a Ph.D. from UCLA, but also the principal owner of the Metro Computer store in downtown Los Angeles and the Byte Shop computer store in Brentwood, a Los Angeles suburb. Both stores sell home and small business computers. The Brentwood shop is on the ground floor of a modern glass-enclosed office building. Its orange counters and stalls are arranged in a series of triangles, utilizing every corner and wall of the store. The software is stacked in racks, like brochures in a travel agency, and on flat desks sit the hardware, the computers and video screens costing from $300 to $10,000.

The home computer industry is new, perhaps five years old at the most. Unlike many other products, a computer is not bought on impulse. Customers, in fact, need a thorough orientation before they can begin to understand the value of having their own computer. In a real sense, Jim Roseboro is in the education business.

Roseboro markets several kinds of home and small business computers. Most of these consist of a keyboard resembling a medium-size typewriter, a box reading the floppy disks that contain programs, and a video monitor (although most computers can be hooked up to any television set). He has been selling computers like these for four years, and each year sales go up.

The story of Jim Roseboro, the scientist and the businessman, begins in 1941 in Charlotte, North Carolina, where he was born the oldest son in a black family. His father was a truck mechanic and worked steadily all his life, which gave the family stability. Both parents, though relatively uneducated, believed ardently in schooling. As a child Jim had some severe illnesses and came close to dying more than once. Today, he stands six feet and three inches tall and looks like he could have played professional football.

In Roseboro's senior year at West Charlotte High School, Dorothy Counts became the first black to attend classes at a neighboring high school, a tumultuous event for the community and for him. Dorothy Counts was often insulted by mobs of whites but continued to attend and ultimately graduated. The barriers were coming down, and Roseboro was to become actively involved in the civil rights movement in Charlotte.

After high school Jim won academic scholarships to several colleges and decided to attend the University of Detroit. After completing a year, he dropped out and took a job with the federal government as a mathematics aide. He also worked with the American Express Company for a while, but he soon came to realize that he needed and wanted more education.

"I enrolled at Johnson C. Smith University in Charlotte, a predominantly black school with 1,200 students. It was there that I took a course in radiation biology and first became aware of radiation hazards." He graduated with a degree in mathematics and physics in 1965.

"It was a big year, the year of the urban riots and mass marches, all of which added to my commitment to social change. I was involved with the early sit-ins and became a writer for a magazine called *The Moderator*, sponsored by the National Student Association. It crystalized my will to make a difference.

"With my degree in math and physics, I took a job with the federal Food and Drug Administration, Bureau of Radiological Health, working on radiation fallout studies. At the time both the Russians and Americans were conducting atmospheric nuclear testing. Our work was devoted to defining fallout patterns in the United States and its territories. We found that fallout was concentrating in the school food of children in the northern central states. This was the beginning of a deep personal concern about nuclear weapons and their threat to life. I was at the point of applying for marine officer candidate school when my immediate superior in the Bureau of Radiation Health, Robert H. Neal, encouraged me to consider and helped me gain admission to Johns Hopkins University in its radiological sciences program. This was a major turn in my life. I had not expected this opportunity, but once it came the choice was clear. I spent the next two and a half years working on a master's degree and was involved in the design of a facility to test the capacity of small mammals to live in a continuous low-level radiation environment. What I was learning added to my concern about the hazards of radiation and war.

"When I finished work on my degree in 1967, the army offered me a direct commission in the Medical Service Corps, which I took. First, I worked as an assistant to the radiation physicist at Walter

Reed Army Hospital in Washington, D.C., and then spent three years as a nuclear medical science officer at Tripler Army Hospital in Hawaii. When I was relieved from active duty, I was accepted as a doctoral candidate at UCLA.

"While at UCLA, I married Hedi Lang, a Swiss girl, and when I completed the Ph.D. we went to join the faculty at the University of North Carolina. Starting a family added a greater sense of stability and purpose to my life, but I knew that teaching and research were not to be my life's only work. I had a growing sense of wanting to contribute to social change. My ultimate goal was to go into my own business in order to become financially independent and then attempt to influence events. I wanted to contribute more to the changing social scene. To have any influence, one either has to have an extremely strong moral commitment, a moral base, or large material resources. I contrast the kind of commitment that I would have with that, say, of a Dr. Martin Luther King, who was not a wealthy person. His commitment came from a very strong moral base, and he was able to enlist support from substantial people who respected him for his moral position. Not having that strong moral base, I have to build my financial base. That is what led me into business. You need a strong economic foundation to stand on if you are going to challenge established ideas and ways, and I could not gain that financial base in academia."

"The question was what business to go into. Because of my background, I decided to develop a business dealing with high technology. In the early 1970s the microcomputer revolution was getting under way. It really is a revolution. Our technology has made available to the average person the power of a computer, something undreamed of 15 years ago. I had the concept of opening a computer store, and I came back here to Southern California to start it. Southern California is the mecca for high technology advances."

"I interested two partners in the venture, both of whom I had met in the military reserves. There are other businesses that might be lucrative but that have adverse effects on the environment, and I did not want to contribute to that. But computers can have an enormously beneficial influence on the environment. We can measure water and mineral concentrations in the soil by computers and add automatically as needed. Computers can provide an endless variety of such control functions. Through the process of simulation, a computer can take an environmentalist through an entire life span of a plant or animal. Computers contributed to genetic experiments deciphering the DNA."

"Capital investment is a risk," says Roseboro, "but what isn't? What is important is always keeping some options open. I have a part-time teaching position at UCLA. I am also maintaining my research skills by heading a project at Cal Tech/Jet Propulsion Laboratory. That project is looking at alternatives to fumigating fruit to eradicate the medfly."

Roseboro is also a major in the army reserves. The army sends him on special assignments to do radiation studies at its facilities around the world.

When Jim Roseboro gave up a secure academic environment and took on the risks of being an entrepreneur, he left the more manageable flow and pace of Chapel Hill, North Carolina, and plunged into the white water of high tech, trendy southern California. He was able to do this because he has a positive attitude toward risk and change. Far from resisting change, he seeks it, in himself and in the society. To Roseboro change is not something sought for its own sake; it is for a larger purpose. It is also based on a careful reading of the environment and the willingness to move with it.

Asked how he could launch a business without any business or finance experience, he replies, "One thing graduate school does for you is instill confidence. If you weather that storm you feel you can weather almost anything. This business is going to make it, I'm sure. The more it makes it, the more I'm going to work for social change and to educate people about the terrors of radiation sickness in a nuclear war. We cannot envision the horrors of what these weapons will do to civilization, to human beings, to the animal and plant world. I want to influence the people who ultimately make foreign policy and domestic social policy as well. I'm a small voice in the forest, but I think if enough small voices are heard, we can demand of leaders that they not lead us to the abyss."

ROBERT GEORGINE

We next took our search for models to the field of labor. Here, we found a pragmatic, articulate, and flexible leader.

Roughly five feet and ten inches tall, Robert Georgine has the presence of a handsome basso profundo and a smile as big as a quarter moon. His hair is graying, and his handshake is firm and strong enough to convince the visitor that the man has done physically demanding work. Robert Georgine is the president of the Building and Construction Trades Department of the AFL-CIO, which is headquartered in Washington, D.C.

Georgine speaks for a union that represents four and one-half million workers from 15 trades—from electricians to carpenters to plumbers and pipefitters. To join the CIO, a worker needs a job; to join the AFL, a worker has to have mastered a skill. Georgine himself spent a five-year apprenticeship as a lathe metal worker before receiving his union card in 1953.

Born in Chicago in 1932 of Italian descent, Georgine had finished his army service and was a foreman when he first ran for election in the local in 1957. "I was lucky winning as a Georgine in Chicago. The union was as Irish as a population can be outside of Dublin. But I ran because I had some ideas about where the union should go. There were several small recessions in the late 1950s. Work slowed. Collective bargaining issues were becoming more and more important. And I ran because I was a foreman. There was no place to go from foreman. I was married to Mary Rita Greener, the family was on its way, and I was ambitious enough to take my chances in an election."

In 1959 Georgine became a full-time union officer. He has served on the union's executive board, been the assistant business manager, the CIO's representative, the assistant to the president, the secretary-treasurer, and finally its president, winning this position first in 1974 and twice since then.

"If you lose an election," said Georgine, "it's back to the tools," and he looked at his hands. "There've been a lot of changes in my union, but that hasn't changed. You don't get kicked upstairs when you lose an election."

About the changes, Georgine says, "Go back in time. Organized labor had a tough time getting established in Chicago. Management felt that labor unions inhibited its ability to run a business as it wanted, and the workers felt they needed better conditions so they banded together to stop exploitation.

"There were wars between management and labor. Bloody wars. Heads bashed in. Beatings. Murders. When the workers called a strike, management hired strike breakers and scabs. When the workers picketed, management called on the police to disband picket lines. But the working people persevered. There are no more bloody wars."

Georgine believed there was more to life than constant labor-management strife and that growth, jobs, and increased wages for labor were matters of mutual interest. He felt that labor could protect its rights and at the same time work with management. It was this philosophy of cooperation that won him his presidency and that he still pursues today.

However, he is no pushover. On the contrary, he is a dynamic, forceful, and aggressive fighter for labor progress. He works closely with management because it serves to bring benefits that labor deserves. "Growth, productivity, jobs, better living standards, and a better life for all Americans, not only labor—that's my motto," Georgine says. "I am not too stubborn to compromise but my compromises are weighted."

"The struggle still goes on. Management still feels on occasion that a labor union inhibits its ability to run a business as it wants. But anti-union employers these days go after the union with lawyers. Management goes into the courts for injunctions, stays, and the like. Management utilizes laws, sometimes outmoded laws, to entangle and mire the union leadership. Anti-union employers put lobbyists into state legislatures and into Congress to press for laws limiting union tactics. Management delays union elections. And management is often successful in dissuading workers from joining the union. I know that membership in my union does not grow at the ratio that the work force expands.

"A contractor who has signed a collective bargaining agreement with the union is called a 'fair' employer. But if he wins a bid on a project where the engineers and the builder and the owners tell him no union, the contractor simply sets up another company and hires nonunion help. He pays workers top dollar at one end of town and bottom dollar at the other.

"It is costly for a union to keep up with these devices. Organization is expensive but we have to try. So we lobby too. We want the law changed so that strikers in the building trades can picket the entire site. By law we can only picket discrete areas at the present, which means a union member not on strike doesn't have to cross the line to get to work. Other labor unions enjoy the right of full-site picketing, but our union lost it on a court decision in Denver, not in Congress.

"We go to the public, too, over these differences. But an advertisement in a newspaper costs $50,000 for three insertions.

There's a limit to the ads we can run to get our story across. It's difficult. Our opponents are concerted and often we are not. We have to go out and persuade business and management and the public that our product is better, that union members are more efficient, more highly skilled, that this saves costs in the long run and benefits society as a whole.

"This is a big change from the way we conceived tactics 30 and 40 years ago. Technology forced some of these changes. The invention of dry-wall construction alone meant serious changes. Fireproofing a building involves new techniques. Workmen do not have to wrap steel beams as they once did. I have never been convinced that the more intensive the technology, the more work. But right now that is beside the point. We have to change our work rules to remain competitive. And we do change them. The union had a standard clause that the contractor had to install windows in skyscrapers under construction to protect workers from the elements. But we don't put up buildings one story at a time anymore. The contractors argued why did they have to install windows on the thirteenth floor when on the twenty-second the men were working without walls. So we dispensed with the requirement. We told the members that if it is too cold to work, that is management's problem, not ours."

Pointing to his ceiling, Georgine said, "You hang a ceiling with iron or steel hangers. Our contractors used to stipulate that these hangers never be hung more than three feet apart for safety's sake. But the architects and the engineers came up with new ways of hanging ceilings and new alloys; so the contractors went to the union for relief. And the members decided that it was not the union's responsibility to determine safety nor was it equipped to do so. They were there to work, not to police quality.

"Men who worked on the grids of a skeleton skyscraper got more money because their work was dangerous. Management objected to these pay differentials. We agreed with management. No worker anywhere for any reason should work in peril. We gave up the differentials, and management made the grid of the skeleton safe.

"These are some of the technical reasons we change. But we change, too, because there are areas where management and labor have much in common. The union is perfectly well aware that construction in the energy industries has been put off and delayed. We know that a $250 million dollar plant means an expenditure of $500 million for a utility company because of the cost of acquiring money and paying interest for a decade or more. Our workmen could put that plant up in 18 months. It's to our interest. We know that there are 2,000 work hours in a working year of 50 weeks at 40 hours a week. Our members average 1,214 hours a year at $13.00 an hour. We want 2,000 working hours a year. Let us at this construction! We will do anything to help management reduce interest rates, to cut through regulations.

"Management helps us too. Many members of management side with the union in opposing the repeal of the Davis-Bacon Act. Passed in 1931, the act required that contractors engaged in government work pay the prevailing wage of the area to workmen on the project. Congress originally wanted to protect local employers, to keep government money in the local community, to halt the incursion of out-of-area contractors coming in with a cheaper work force. Local communities benefited because the money stayed in town. Workers benefited. Small business doesn't want this act repealed and neither do unions. We do not buy the argument that lower wages mean reduced taxes, which equals prosperity. If you come down to it, the pyramids were built for nothing, but the pyramids were a severe setback for the workers.

"Union members, no less than captains of industry, know that the country has lost its competitive edge in steel and in autos and that the country is not maintaining its competitive advantage in light industry. These industries mean jobs. And if we keep losing this edge, the country's main income will be the money spent by European, Japanese, and Arabian tourists.

"We know that we have to produce the fuels to fire plants for electrical power. The short-term solution is nuclear energy, and the union wants the government to stop impeding the development of nuclear power as much as management does. We know the long-term solution to energy is synfuels, the fuels from coal and shale, and we know this development requires an astronomical capital investment. The developers want the government to guarantee their loans. So does the union."

A brillant and passionate advocate for his cause, Robert Georgine is at the same time a pragmatic and flexible reader of the rapidly changing labor environment.

NORM KING

Business and labor are not the only arenas in which leadership and cooperation can make a difference. The public sector—government—affects each of our lives and certainly our prospects for prosperity.

Palm Springs sits below the mountains covered with chaparral on the broad plain of the California desert. The city is about 100 miles east of Los Angeles. Its buildings, stores, and homes gleam with vivid colors. It is as neatly laid out as a building-block square in a kindergarten.

The town has an official population of 35,000, which swells in the fall and winter months to 70,000 as tourists, golf fanatics, and conventioneers step from jets at the airport as eagerly as prospectors and land agents once stepped down from Wells Fargo stagecoaches.

While the resort atmosphere makes Palm Springs seem special, it has all the problems of other cities and towns in the United States—a wide mix of income, race, and social needs. The relationship of citizens and government is explained with feeling and insight by Norman King, the 38-year-old city manager of this oasis community.

King, good-looking, muscular, with a shock of dark brown hair, white teeth a movie star would envy, and aviator glasses, was born in Bakersfield, California, the son of a school teacher. "I was led to public service," he said, "probably because my father represented that ethic to me. I came out of a town that had hometown values—church, camping trips, high school athletics—which gave me wonderful opportunities."

"When I was graduated from high school, I spent the summer of 1960 in Norway with 1,200 other high school graduates participating in the American Field Service Exchange Student program. This experience opened my eyes, as high school kids like to say." Five years later, King found an even more rewarding experience as an administrator for this program in New York city, his office adjoining the United Nations. He was in charge of U.S. travel operations for foreign students. It was the summer of an airline strike, and charter planes cancelled arrangements. "I was contracting for dozens of buses and losing kids from Thailand with names as long as a legal contract."

King, a graduate of Claremont McKenna College, a small, private school in California, went to the Wharton School at the University of Pennsylvania for a master's degree in government administration. After an internship in the city manager's office in Ontario, California, he returned to Claremont for his first job.

"I was in front of the baby boom. When I got a job in Claremont, there were many openings in public service; five years later, there weren't. Once the population reached its crest, new workers filled up the openings quickly. But in my time, career expectations were quickly realized.

"I went from administrative assistant to city manager in about six years. And I went forward in a time when citizens had a good deal more confidence in city government. When I first started work, I was involved in a campaign to raise $6 million in bonds for various city projects ranging from a library to a park to a railroad crossing. The city had to have the approval of two-thirds of the registered voters to issue a general obligation bond, but we achieved this vote with little opposition. It is not possible to issue general obligation bonds today.

"Things were easier in the 1960s. People were more willing to let City Hall make decisions. Ten years ago, Clarement decided to widen a street. There were citizens who argued this would destroy the Claremont mystique, that the town was a small one that could do without a four-lane street with a center island. But these voices were not insistent. At a public meeting attended by 300 citizens, the council took a vote and went ahead with the project. Today with its trees and its ability to circulate traffic, the street and island are a community asset. If Claremont tried this now, opponents would threaten to circulate a recall petition unseating council members. Few of these opponents would understand the value of community-wide traffic circulation. Before the council attempted to widen a street, it would have to produce professional engineering studies and devote full-time efforts to persuading groups who can concentrate every energy on blocking such a proposal.

"Fifteen years ago, when citizens disagreed with the decisions of local government, they still believed that government had a rationale, that the mayor and the council and the manager weren't harebrained. Citizens do not believe this today. Cities and towns now deal with single-issue constituencies that often are powerful enough to dissuade councils from making wise decisions.

"Recently, an entrepreneur came to the Palm Springs Planning

Commission wanting to know what conditions he would have to meet to construct a six-story luxury hotel in an area marked for redevelopment. Six stories is the maximum height the city will allow. Would the city approve this? He wanted to know what he could expect. To what zoning and environmental laws did he have to conform? Before he put up the front money for architectural plans and land acquisition, he wanted to know what his chances were. It was a perfectly reasonable request. It was sound business practice. But this land adjoined a prestige neighborhood. Before you knew it, we had petitions and lawyers in here. Everyone acted on the assumption that the city had already approved construction of the new hotel. Everyone charged that the democratic process has been bypassed. This forced the developer to back off from even having his plans reviewed. The land is still undeveloped, although a hotel would provide the city with tax revenue.

"If you work in government, you're fair game for criticism. Public employees work on the principle that the citizen is always right, and unwarranted criticism is sometimes hard to handle. It is particularly hard when the public will not come directly to government to relieve its grievances. If there's a dead tree endangering a street, city hall may learn about it from a letter to the editor. One wonders sometimes if the intent is to remedy the hazard or simply to make city hall look bad. It is frustrating to think that the very people you are committed to serve as a public servant sometimes think of you as an enemy.

"When the council takes the bit in its teeth and votes for an unpopular decision, even the courts try to second-guess its action. In the past the courts shied from reviewing the decisions of a duly elected body unless that decision was unconstitutional or inequitable. But more and more, the courst are weighing the merits of purely political decisions.

"One of the radical and unfortunate changes is that citizens and governments have come to consider themselves adversaries. And the reason for this is that many citizens simply do not know enough about local government. They love their community and have a 'feel' for it, but they do not understand how even a small city is a complex interconnected organism. Seemingly minor decisions often involve difficult trade-offs with other values and ideals.

"One of the reasons that people and government are adversaries, perhaps the compelling reason, evolves from what people want from their government. What people want is *more*—more facilities, more schools, more parks, more parking, more protection. When these aren't forthcoming, people complain that government is unresponsive. But governments are too responsive. That's why many city and state governments are broke.

"The campaign talk that promises smaller government is rhetoric. You can't sit through as many public meetings as I do and draw any other conclusion. You never hear people in city council meetings asking for less government. For example, the constituency wants a risk-free community, but a risk-free town is very expensive. No one hires a lifeguard for a private swimming pool, although certainly there are risks attendant with swimming in a private pool. But if the city builds a municipal pool, it has to have more than one lifeguard and maybe even a nurse.

"Again: sensibly enough, people want a pollution-free environment. And it is possible to achieve a 95 percent control of pollutants. But when the constitutency insists on 100 percent, they fail to realize that the costs aren't 5 percent more, but often 50 percent more or even double. Dealing with the issues day in and day out, year in and year out, I believe that 100 percent solutions defy us; at least the costs do. But if the city doesn't solve a problem 100 percent, it is as though it hasn't solved it at all.

"I think of this as a 'God is Dead' attitude. People once accepted a legal principle that there were 'Acts of God'—a flood or a tornado. But people, or at least the courts, do not accept this principle anymore. There are no more acts of God—someone is always held responsible for the catastrophe. In most cases it's the city, which is bound to be financially responsible for the damage wreaked by a riot, for example. In California, even when the court determines that a city is only 5 percent responsible for a liability claim, it is not uncommon that the city will have to pay 50 percent or more on the award. There are many other situations in which cities are being held liable, which means more government, not less, because government must provide the increased protection or service or pay for any damages.

"You know, the percentage of government expenditures that has risen alarmingly has not been in the traditional areas of road maintenance or police protection, but in grants to individuals, to lawyers who defend the town, and to insurance companies. Some social and service costs of these kinds are necessary but the benefits are not visible to people."

City managers in California—and King is no exception—are exercised by any discussion about Proposition 13. Proposition 13 was an initiative voted in by Californians in 1976 halting the acceleration of property taxes. Property values had suffered a disquieting appreciation as cities and towns and counties expanded, an appreciation in value that raised some homeowners' taxes as high as their mortgage payments. In many respects a necessary curb, Proposition 13 still inflicts certain inequities. A newer homeowner may pay double the taxes his neighbor, an older resident, pays. But the passage of this initiative forced urgent changes and innovations on local governments.

"In addition to the inequities created between owners of like properties," King said, "Proposition 13 is shifting property taxes more to residential property because houses turn over more frequently than business property. What Proposition 13 has done to this desk," he said, gesturing, "is make financial planning for the future virtually impossible. It was supposed to make government more efficient, but efficiency entails long-range financial planning. No city can do this if it's unsure of its financial base.

"For a time after Proposition 13 was passed, the state of California provided bail-out money to cities. This is no longer the case; in fact, cities face the prospect of a reverse bail-out. Most cities have had to cut spending considerably.

"In this economic climate, there is a tendency to take a short-term view by deferring maintenance expenditures. I urged the council not to mortgage the future in this way. I am gratified that both in Claremont and Palm Springs the city councils took the difficult step of cutting programs rather than deferring maintenance. They realized that deferring maintenance is not a savings; the costs are simply shifted to future taxpayers.

"Proposition 13 weakened local control over local government. Once the state legislature gave a city discretionary money—that is, money not earmarked for a specific purpose—the legislature asked questions: Does this city need it more than another city? In what ways will the city spend this money? Let's say for reasons of its own, a city wanted to expand a specific service to a higher level than other cities. This could raise conflicts with the state, which seems to be moving to impose mandatory minimum and maximum levels of services, thus limiting local government discretion.

"The federal government also has a growing impact on cities. Whether it's a project undertaken by the Army Corps of Engineers or a transportation grant, federal agencies set standards of safety, employment, and access which affect every community. It all adds up to less local control, less ability for local citizens to decide things for themselves.

"So you can see how Proposition 13 had a centralizing effect in California. The local citizen and his elected representatives on the council have far less discretion over funds and a lessening ability in planning what's good for the community."

Asked about the process of change and adaptation, King says, "First of all, we city managers have to rid ourselves of the expectations of the 1950s and 1960s. The reality is that cities have new and severe financial and resource constraints. We cannot wave these away. We know these constraints induce frustration.

"More and more local government is called upon to be a broker, to negotiate among regional, state, or federal agencies on service systems. City managers are not usually trained as negotiators, but we have to negotiate with these agencies to protect the city from overregulation and from the installation of overly expensive systems.

"We need to have a systems view. We need to look at a total system to manage demand as well as supply of public services. Let me give you an example. Traditionally, cities have met the need for fire protection by supplying more firemen. Building and manning new firehouses entails an astronomical cost. We passed an ordinance in Palm Springs a few years ago that requires a sprinkler system in residential as well as commercial structures built outside a five-minute response from the nearest fire station. We have found that sprinklers are efficient in houses and more than pay for themselves. Admittedly, government has imposed an additional cost on builders, but we have imposed it to effect economies in the long run.

"The sprinkler system has solved a problem by redefining it. The original problem was how to get enough firemen to fires quickly enough to contain them. Our fire chief rethought the problem by asking, 'How can we insure that fires do not get out of control as quickly?'

"Trying to reduce demand before increasing supply applies to other problems as well. Consider waste disposal. It costs more and more money to acquire property for landfills. Acreage for sanitary landfills is diminishing in urban areas; collection is expensive. If we redefine the problem, we realize straight off that there's too much trash to begin with. We have to invent ways to reduce refuse. Some states have passed 'bottle bills' that require a deposit on every bottle or can, paid back to the customer when the bottle or can is returned for recycling. This is an illustration of government reducing the demand for a public service.

"Government has to spend less time worrying about traditional systems and respond to change by evolving new systems. Preventive medicine is more sensible and cheaper than providing more and more hospital beds.

"Lastly, let me make a point about the uniqueness, the individual quality of cities. In Palm Springs a large percentage of the land is Indian-owned. The Agua Caliente Indians have lived in the Palm Springs area for centuries. In 1896 the federal government allocated the land in one-mile square sections in a checkerboard fashion, one-half of the checkerboard squares to the tribe, the other half to the Southern Pacific Railroad. Over the years much of the railroad land was sold to private developers, and most of the development and growth took place on non-Indian land. Some low-cost marginal development such as trailer parks were placed on some of the Indian land, but most Indian-owned land remained undeveloped.

"In the 1950s most of the Indian land was allocated to some 150 individual members of the Agua Caliente tribe. Beginning in the 1960s the Department of Interior finally began to allow long-term leases on Indian-owned land, thus facilitating many major new developments that have been built or are under construction. The Indian-owned land, by federal policy, is exempt from local zoning ordinances if the local tribal council votes to overturn the city ordinance or zoning plan. Even the California Environmental Protection Act does not apply to Indian-owned land if the tribal council does not wish to abide by it. This history and situation obviously breeds a certain amount of distrust and conflict which both the tribal council and the city council are trying hard to minimize.

"There is no right or wrong in the situation. I mention it only to illustrate that every city has its own unique mix of social, physical, and economic conditions. That is what makes city management so vital. If you think about it, that is the strength of this country, along with the fact that it is always changing."

JOSIE BAIN

Society adapts to change by virtue of its ability to educate and re-educate its citizens, and it is to that field of education that we turn for the subject of our next profile.

Dr. Josie Bain's house sits on the bluff of one of Los Angeles's hills. Wall-length picture windows reveal a panoramic view of the San Fernando Valley. The view is inspirational.

Dr. Bain is a black woman in her sixties, her hair barely tinged with gray. She is extremely vigorous, to which her handshake testifies. She walks and talks like a woman in supreme health. Her smile is open and confident. Her home reflects this openness. From the foyer, one can see the expanse of three generous rooms furnished in exquisite taste.

Dr. Bain recently retired as associate superintendent of instruction for the Los Angeles Unified School District, the second largest public school system in our country. The district encompasses some 710 square miles, hundreds of schools, and hundreds of thousands of pupils speaking dozens of languages. She now serves on the state board of education and is a consultant for the state personnel board, as well as a member of two corporate boards. This is a remarkable accomplishment for a woman who was born in poverty in the years just prior to World War I—the eighth of nine children of a Methodist parson in Georgia. "My schooling was rudimentary," she says. "Teachers in those years in Georgia didn't need much certification. A few years of schooling qualified a student as a teacher. However, after completing elementary school in Atlanta, I went to Oglethorpe High School. This was what we now call a private school. The children here, though not affluent, were the children of black lawyers and doctors and undertakers, and they knew they were going on in life. At first I couldn't compete, but I stuck to it. When I didn't understand the assignment, I stayed after school and asked again and again. My teachers seemingly took a personal interest. I learned I could hold my own. I finished high school.

"About this time I met John Bain, a young theological student in his senior year at Gammon Theological Seminary and married him when I was 16. Marrying him was a wise decision. I learned from him how to deal with people and be comfortable with them. While he was finishing his work at Gammon Seminary, I went to

Williams Business College and learned typing. I didn't have a typewriter at home; so when the day was over, I stayed on, practicing for an hour or longer. This skill stayed me well in subsequent years.

"Our first assignment in the ministry was in Springhill, Tennessee, a three-point county circuit. John tended to three different churches. On the fourth Sunday everyone—Baptists, Methodists, Disciples of Christ—collected at one church, a get-together for everyone. Church was the social agency, the spiritual anchor, the inspiration for blacks at this time, holding the community together.

"After the birth of my first child, we moved to Murfreesboro, Tennessee, where I went 60 miles every week to Tennessee State College, with John taking care of the baby. I was striving for a Normal Degree, equivalent to an A.A. today. My husband attended full-time during the summer. We evidently impressed the college president, because he offered John the position of chaplain at the college. We spent the next two years on the second floor of a dormitory cooking on a two-eye electric plate, washing clothes in the bathtub, housed in two small rooms with the bathroom located on the first floor.

"In 1938 we were assigned to Des Moines, Iowa; so my husband could continue his education at Drake University. When I felt left out, he said, 'We'll both go.' He went to the graduate, and I went to the undergraduate school. After one semester we knew we couldn't afford it. I went to the dean, who said since I was one of the first black married students on the campus, he'd secure a scholarship which would pay all my tuition—if I stayed on the honor roll. I did my part and the dean did his. In two years I was graduated, and my husband was awarded his master's degree. We were the first black couple to be graduated from Drake University. John and I feel we served as catalysts for other blacks, for Drake has made great strides in opening its doors to black students since that time.

"When the war came John wanted to serve as a chaplain. He felt he had an obligation to young men leaving their homes for the first time, and he enlisted. When he received an overseas assignment, I was left alone with our 12-year-old son."

One feels Josie Bain's deep commitment to family, as well as a strong sense of "I will," a quality that undoubtedly husband and wife nourished in each other. She moved to Los Angeles and found a job as a typist for the army. Although an army installation staffed by whites was located within walking distance of her home, Josie had to take several buses to her office across town. "No one thought blacks could work alone among whites, or 'Anglos' as they are often called in Los Angeles." Eventually, Josie was promoted to a position in the employee relations section, a real breakthrough since no blacks had been serving in such a position in that army installation. She remained in this position, a role model and an inspiration to minorities, until her husband returned.

"After John returned from the war, we spent a year in Springfield, Missouri, where he served as minister at the Methodist church. Our parsonage was hardly a desirable place to live. Rats ran around in the attic at night as if holding a convention. The town itself was stagnant. When my son saw it for the first time, upon our arrival in Springfield, he asked, 'Where are the lights?' But we settled down to getting rid of the rats and making other changes and always looking up. I got a job as a substitute teacher. I had always wanted to be a teacher, and this was a beginning.

"In 1946 we were able to return to Los Angeles when my husband was offered a parish in the recently organized Bower Memorial Methodist Church. This gave our son the chance to go to UCLA. I still wanted to teach more than anything else, and my experience as a substitute teacher and my training qualified me for the Los Angeles school system. I was warned by friends that the board of educational hired few blacks, but I went anyway. In the personnel office a little Anglo girl said, 'You can't take the exam; you don't have the needed background, and furthermore we don't have any openings for you.' With that she rather abruptly ended our conversation. I thought, How am I going to get around this? When I started to leave I saw a name on a door—H. H. Baldwin, personnel chief. Returning to the office, I said to the girl that Mr. Baldwin had cleared me for the examination, and I couldn't understand why she was denying me this opportunity. The name Baldwin changed her attitude completely, and I was given the necessary forms to complete. Remember, I really had never seen Mr. Baldwin, nor he me.

"When I came home, John asked what would I have done if Mr. Baldwin had walked in at that moment. I said that I would have told him I was the girl he talked with three weeks ago. 'All blacks look alike,' I said, 'and I don't think Mr. Baldwin would have known the difference.' I passed the test and I started as a first grade teacher at Marianna Avenue Elementary School in the heart of a Mexican-American barrio."

Motivated by a clear goal, Josie Bain persevered not only against poverty and prejudice, but against the belief that what she was trying to do was "too hard." She was a victim of circumstances, which is never pleasant, but she did not lash out in anger against those who tried to hold her back. She accepted conditions as they were and worked with them, through them, and at times around them.

Then there was a turn in the tide. In the postwar years California's population and economy burgeoned, and more workers were needed to fill many new jobs. For the first time, blacks could aspire to the middle class through civil service. Thousands of blacks were attending colleges on the GI Bill. A significant number of blacks were raising another generation bound for the professions, and expectations were rising.

"In my first years at the predominantly Hispanic school," she said, "I acquired the methodology to back up my knowledge. Two years after I started, I was asked to develop a training program for principals. Many of the principals at that time were men who had taught only at the upper elementary or high school level. They weren't adequately prepared to help a kindergarten or first-grade teacher. It takes some training to get second graders into the yard in organized play instead of running wild. My program was successful and my supervisor encouraged me to go into administration. I took the vice-principal's examination and passed and was appointed as vice-principal at the new San Jose Elementary School, which had been built for 500 students and opened with 1,600.

"I found extraordinary help from the faculty and administration there. My principal told me one day that while she knew I was enjoying my stay, there were principals, perhaps, with whom I would not be able to relate. She insisted I take the principal's examination and backed me all the way. I was successful, finishing in the top ten, and soon I was assigned as the principal at the Albion Elementary School off North Broadway, a school made up largely of Mexican-American and black kids.

"I saw immediately that these kids were really not getting a fair chance. The teachers often went to the lounge when they came in rather than going to their classrooms to prepare for the day. Having been a teacher, I knew you couldn't walk into the school unprepared and teach 40 kids. So I set standards. We had a goodly number of transfers—which was precisely what I wanted, because those who transferred were old-timers who either wanted to run the school, disliked a black person telling them what to do, or both. My concern was for the children and how little we were doing for them. I instituted training programs for the teachers. We had musical programs involving the entire community. We changed the academic climate at Albion, and those who stayed felt good about what was happening."

After seven years Bain was promoted to administrative coordinator for the North Area, an area carved out of the center of Los Angeles. Two years later she was again promoted, this time to area superintendent for the area that included Watts. After the riots in 1965, she had tremendous difficulty in recruiting teachers.

"When school opened in September, I had classrooms with no teachers. We scrounged for substitutes, and we hired anybody with a college degree. This was a very discouraging time because we knew the kids were being short-changed. We had many, many teachers teaching out of their field of training. We had others who lacked commitment and were using this only as a stepping stone.

"We had children in the third grade who didn't know how to hold a book, children who couldn't write their names. Many of them lacked motivation, and those who had ability had little or no encouragement at home. I convened panels of principals and teachers to think this problem through and instituted programs that enjoyed moderate success. We succeeded in getting highly skilled and efficient teachers to go into the schools as model teachers to move from class to class, helping new teachers and letting them observe appropriate methods.

"We began testing for academic proficiency in the first grade instead of the eleventh and twelfth when actually it's too late. We continued this to determine whether or not our teaching techniques were proving successful.

"In order to give the community insight and the opportunity to participate in the total program, we initiated a Fine Arts Festival where children's literature and art were displayed. The superintendent of schools managed to reserve the Music Center where we filled the stage. That program gave better than 1,000 children the opportunity to perform the finest music of the world. We were able to get the most attractive and prestigious spot in Los Angeles for that presentation—the Dorothy Chandler Pavilion of the Music Center. Better than 4,000 parents and children participated in and gave support to this idea which became an annual event. Nothing of this magnitude had taken place before in the district.

"We sought new and creative ways to meet the needs of an extremely diverse student body. Our goals were not fully met, but parents had been turned on; principals and teachers felt there was backing, support, and direction. We were beginning to blossom."

In the midst of success and change, Bain was moved to affluent West Los Angeles. Again, there was the need to prove herself. The area was very different. Here, people were committed to education, and they demanded excellence for their children. For the most part, the children were highly motivated. It was a test of whether she could function in this area or whether her skills were limited to working with parents lacking in academic background.

"Regardless of area or background, all parents want the best for their kids. I followed the same philosophy that every child is entitled to an education within the range of his or her capability and we got the same positive results."

As she approached retirement age, Bain was again moved up, this time to associate superintendent of instruction for the entire Los Angeles Unified District. For most this would have been a natural progression, but for Josie Bain, a black, a woman, and one who by this time had developed a reputation for being tough and sometimes 'aggressive,' it was a surprise to many people. She adjusted to working with all men and once again met with success.

"How do I account for the progress from the eighth of nine children, born into poverty, growing up in a totally segregated and unequal society, to the position of associate superintendent of instruction in the second largest school district in our country and the highest paid woman? First, I had a sense of personal self-worth instilled by a mother who refused to let the circumstances of the day set limits for her children. There was always the challenge of a better day, but each must be prepared, including Josie. Secondly, I was willing to work hard, staying with a given task until it was completed. Lastly, I had hopes, and hope is the beginning of movement. Hope gives one the will and determination to use all available resources, including people, to achieve a given level of service.

"The education process is now under attack from all corners. Almost everyone went to school one time; so almost everyone knows how best it ought to be run. It will survive if a commitment to quality education moves beyond rhetoric to adequate funding. California now ranks fiftieth in the amount of personal income directed to education."

There is urgency and clarity of purpose in Josie Bain's voice today. In her heart she is a teacher, and the education of children will always come first. As a member of the state board of education, she still gives input to the process.

CHARLES PETERS, JR.

Socrates called himself a gadfly, telling the jurors in the *Apology* that the Delphic oracle had commanded him to irritate the Athenians, not cheer them up. Charles Peters, Jr. is exactly the same gadfly in contemporary Washington, D.C.

Peters is the publisher and editor in chief of the *Washington Monthly*, whose subject is government and the inability of government to govern. While the *Monthly* includes some of the most accurate investigative reporting written today, it is devoted neither to the traditional forms of muckraking nor to exposés. It concentrates on the *process* of government rather than its aim, reporting the actual disposition of Congress, the judiciary, the White House, the press, and elected and appointed bureaucratic officials, rather than on the ideal each professes.

"It is one thing," says Peters, "to report on the passage of an important law and to explicate its provisions; that is done every day. It is another to report on what the law means to constituents in Terre Haute and Newark. Sometimes laws unwittingly provoke hardship. And many laws are never implemented."

The *Washington Monthly* describes not only what government thinks it is doing, but also what it is not doing. In 1981 it ran articles on the actual working schedules of Department of Labor employees. It looked at the Office of Civil Rights and reported that many of the civil rights complaints were filed by agency employees against the agency itself. It revealed that the federal government's "lease-construct" policy for acquiring office space costs taxpayers 2.5 times more than constructing its own buildings and leaves taxpayers with nothing at the end of 20 years.

Peters, at 55 years of age, is portly and handsome, with wavy silver hair. His soft southern accent identifies him as a West Virginian. After graduation from Columbia College in 1949 and a brief stint in television, Peters went to the University of Virginia where he earned a law degree in 1957. After marrying Beth Hubbell, he returned to his father's law firm in Charleston, and in 1959 he ran for the state legislature. "Running is an understatement," he said. "In 1959 the candidates were listed in alphabetical order. One of my notable accomplishments was to become the first 'p' to serve in the legislature from Charleston.

"In 1960 I was John Kennedy's campaign manager in the crucial West Virginia presidential primary. It was a crucial event in my life, too, because in 1961, Kennedy appointed me legal counsel for the newly created Peace Corps. I wanted a political career—I had hopes one day of running for governor—and the chance to be in at the birth of the New Frontier certainly advanced that prospective career.

"In the beginning I worked for the Peace Corps on a per diem basis. One of the jobs to which I gravitated was evaluation of how the new programs worked. The Peace Corps was launched with a burst of enthusiasm. It had a kind of press which constantly expatiated on the sacrifice and altruism of the volunteers, rather than on the value of the program itself.

"But I was the staff member who was constantly in the field, and there was a world of difference between the self-congratulations passing back and forth across desks in Washington and the complaints and despair of young people in strange surroundings.

"Government in Washington is self-centered. The men and women who work in this company town are insulated from what actually transpires. They worry about operations out there only in terms of good or bad publicity. There's some excuse for this. Communications from the field are always sparse and almost always censored: the field boss isn't always anxious to tell his Washington superior that matters are proceeding less than smoothly.

"I short-circuited this. For example, I found that of 61 volunteers in Pakistan, 46 were absolutely idle; their technical skills, command of language, and knowledge of the host country were inadequate. It was a demoralizing experience for these young men and women volunteers who had high hopes of bettering matters. And Pakistan wasn't a unique situation; it was typical. So I sent my reports directly to Sargent Shriver, the head of the program, bypassing my superiors. I knew Shriver was an honest man; as a former journalist he appreciated clean and concise writing. And Shriver responded. Eventually, every Washington-based staff member had to read the reports.

"At the end of several months, I went back to West Virginia, but the Peace Corps called on me again and again for evaluative reports and finally asked me to come aboard as a permanent member. I stayed there for seven years, during which time I realized that I was not going to be the governor of West Virginia.

"I was fascinated by the way a federal agency works and how government organizations go about their tasks. I had a far different perspective from that of the ordinary citizen. The top of the organization simply never wants to know about the myriad problems at the base. A government organization is in the business of persuading the client, who is Congress or the president or the public, that everything is fine. That has become the organization's raison d'être. The details of specific problems never go up the line. This isn't the nature of Washington agencies and bureaus only, but the nature of agencies and bureaus everywhere.

"In Vietnam General Koster kept dispatching his aide Colonel Henderson to find out exactly what happened at My Lai. And the colonel kept telling the general, 'Nothing out of the ordinary.' But any general who wants to know what's happening in the field goes out and asks a sergeant or a corporal. Never ask the people who know what you want to hear.

"That is why I started the magazine, to make people listen to what they didn't hear or what they didn't want to hear or kept themselves from hearing. I wanted to apply my principle of evaluation to the government as a whole.

"I was perfectly well aware that the magazine business was a more hazardous living than managing a restaurant. But optimistically I thought the *Monthly* would catch on faster than it did. I had to mortgage and remortgage the house to keep the magazine going." The Peters's modest home is in the northwest area of Washington, just past Georgetown. It is whitewashed brick, narrow, and three stories high. The living room table is piled high with manuscripts, galley proofs, and memoranda.

In 1976 the *Washington Monthly* won the Annual Polk Award for newsworthy reporting for its detailed revelations of the U.S. Army's policy of keeping dossiers on politically active citizens.

"One of the faults of Washington government," said Peters, "is that there is no one to make sure that an order is executed exactly as it was given. President Lyndon Johnson asked the army to assume a riot-control role in the 1960s. He did not order the army to discover who might or might not incite riots, only to prepare itself to quell riots. The army took on more than it was asked to take on, to its consequent embarrassment. The duty of the army, and I quote eminent authorities, is to protect citizens from incursions and attacks by a foreign power, not engage in warlike activities against its own people.

"Something important happened to me," said Peters. "I was inside the system, and when I came out I had nothing important to snitch about or expose, but I had seen the system at work. Systems often work the way they do because of the vast cynicism of the system's workers and the incredible naiveté of the people for whom the system is organized. The culture of the bureaucracy needs more thoroughgoing research than any culture in the Trobriand Islands. If you examine the anthropological aspect of government rather than its economic aspect, you will find venality is not the main problem. More trouble is generated by cynics trying to advance their careers from Grade 12 to 13 than by Congressmen taking bribes; more woe results from the tenure of the inefficient than from sporadic sorties of men on the take."

In 1980 Peters published *How Washington Really Works* (Addison-Wesley), an examination of how the judiciary, press, Congress, Foreign Service, and national defense industries operated behind the scenes. The book lent further prestige to the *Monthly*, which presently has a circulation of 34,000, 75 percent of whom are journalists, teachers of government, or government officials. The *Washington Monthly* has proved an exemplar to periodicals more prestigious than itself; the *Washington Post* and the *New York Times*, for example, run one or two stories a week about the operations of government. Before the *Monthly* was established they ran at most one a month. Former *Monthly* reporters have gone on to influential editorial jobs at *The New Yorker*, *Esquire*, and *Harper's*, among others.

Peters says, "Everything I have seen has made me concerned at the lack of entrepreneurial spirit in large bureaucratic organizations, whether private or public—the lack of drive to put over a product whether it's a car or a social service. People in large organizations seem to have focused on the fear of failure. The key to a more vital economy is to forget failure, forget the fear that invests it. We need civil servants and presidents, economists and reporters who are adventurous and willing to take risks to bring about beneficial ends. We need leaders who are willing to face the shame of being wrong."

Charles Peters lives his philosophy of risk taking. He has everything on the line, running his magazine devoted to reforming and changing the huge organization of the government from the outside.

ANDY LIPKIS

The U.S. working population embraces a variety of sectors—business, government, education, and so on. But one area of endeavor that requires unparalleled dedication is volunteer work, and it is from the ranks of the nonprofit volunteer organizations that our next model emerges.

Andy Lipkis, 28 years old, is the head of Tree People, a unique volunteer environmental and conservation organization. The Tree People's central project is to plant one million trees in Los Angeles before the 1984 Olympics. Lipkis has recruited thousands of volunteers for this project to add to the urban forest. The urban forest is his idea and consuming passion. Short of banishing cars from the freeways and shutting down factories, the urban forest is one of the most effective ways of reducing smog in Los Angeles.

"Trees came into my life in the tenth grade," Lipkis said. "I went to a camp run by the Jewish Centers Association in the San Bernardino mountains. That summer the Forest Service announced that smog was killing 40,000 trees a year in the local forest. By 1995 there wouldn't be any trees on the slopes of those mountains. After learning of the problem, we kids decided to make a summer project out of planting smog-tolerant trees. Twenty-four of us tore up the tar on an old parking lot, built stone walls, and planted trees. The friendships we formed in that effort were incredibly strong.

"When I got back to high school, I enrolled in an innovative program, under the guidance of a graduate biologist from UCLA, that taught me how to do research about trees. I began to plan a project, a summer camp where kids could come up for two weeks or a month to plant trees. I realized soon enough this was impractical, but then I thought kids already in summer camps could plant trees. I even went to the offices of a major oil company that had promoted their product as improving the environment. I told their PR man how the smog was killing the trees. He listened and advised me that if the trees were dying, it was because of the smog coming from Kaiser Steel and that my course of action was to organize the workers there to force management to clean up their pollution. I ate this advice up, but by the time I reached the sidewalk, I realized I'd been had, that the guy simply wanted me out of there, and this realization so upset me that I quit—for a time. I've learned a lot since then."

Tree People, which is the organization's incorporated name, has its headquarters on top of the Hollywood Hills in Los Angeles. The headquarters consists of several buildings. The site was once a mountain fire patrol headquarters, and the original horse stables are still there. One of these buildings has been converted into a front office, another into a classroom. The stables and garages house an impressive stock of tools, soil, and plants. Two solar heating units, a vegetable garden, a chicken coop, and two compost piles, which steam like a Turkish bath, have been added to the site. On the surrounding slopes of these 32 acres are herb gardens, a water fountain with the legend "Do you know where this water comes from?" scratched in the concrete, and a system of stone retainer walls built by convicts in the 1930s. The area has the feeling of a restful park.

"When I didn't get my idea for a summer camp going, I went off to Sonoma State College, but I got restless there and finally got sick and was in bed for 5 days. It is when I get sick and then totally rested that I get my life-guiding ideas. I decided to get trees, take them to camps where the kids were, present educational programs, and plant the trees. I got one of my professors at Sonoma State to sponsor me in an independent study project. I found a list of all the camps in the mountains, sent a mailer to them, and got 20 responses. We needed 20,000 trees to plant, and I found 20,000 trees at a State Department of Forestry Nursery at Davis. The trees were scheduled to be plowed under because the state didn't have the resources to plant them and no one had bought them. The law said the trees couldn't be given away, and the 20,000 cost $800, which I didn't have.

"I took off from school and went to Los Angeles when they began killing the trees. I talked to people in Senator Cranston's office, to an assemblyman in Los Angeles, and to a reporter at the *Los Angeles Times*. The reporter verified that indeed the state was plowing under these needed trees. The paper put pressure on the governor in Sacramento by threatening to run a story: 'State Kills Baby Trees,' and a loophole was soon found in the law. Forestry officials flew down to talk to me and promised me 100 trees, which I said weren't enough. Finally, after seeing that I knew what to do, they agreed to send me all of the surviving trees, 8,000 of them. They came to the house I was sharing with other students at Sonoma State. They were bare root trees, about 1,000 to a box the size of a foot locker.

"They had to be refrigerated immediately, then potted in milk cartons, and planted within ten days. Sonoma State stored some of the trees in their refrigerator, and a dormitory cafeteria took another 3,000. Foster's Freeze, which was next door to my house, took a thousand and we took the rest. College students helped pot the trees, and we worked all day and all night. When we realized we needed more people, we called the Boy Scouts, and when that wasn't enough, we called the Girl Scouts.

"We got them potted in ten days, but then we had to get them from Sonoma to Los Angeles. The *Times* reporter wrote a story, 'Andy Versus the Bureaucratic Dead Wood,' which concluded with my estimate that we needed 50 cents per tree to get them into the ground. People started calling at seven o'clock the next morning. Little kids sent their lunch money. Businessmen contributed $100 checks. With my family's help, I created a nonprofit organization called the California Conservation Project. I hired five friends and we got the trees trucked down to Los Angeles, and the camp kids planted them in the mountains. We told kids where smog came from and that, at that moment, they were the only ones doing anything to save the forest from dying.

"Those who worked in the project learned a vital truth—people will identify with a positive solution to a problem, and they will work hard for it. This kind of work creates energy and excitement; so you don't get tired.

"I came to realize that our society is like one big restaurant—the Cafe U.S.A. Our elected representatives, mayors, governors, senators, members of congress, and state legislators are like waiters and waitresses, but instead of summoning them and asking for specific actions we only complain and grow angry that society isn't giving us what we want.

"The first year of the tree project generated thousands and thousands of letters to the governor, legislators, and city council members. The letters were from people who simply wanted to save the forest. Some kids only drew a picture of the forest or made a tape in class of a poem or song about the trees. I believe all those thousands of letters have had a major impact on a wide range of environmental legislation. Working with people in planting trees, I have a feeling we might be getting a solution to the smog problem just by continuing to plant trees and teach people, that is, to awaken and activate people. People don't need to be taught as much as they need support in getting involved.

"The Planning Department and the Air Quality Management District are concerned with the purity of Los Angeles air. They had discovered that in Dayton, Ohio, and in Stuttgart, Germany, the planting of trees created air flows in the city to flush the air. These two agencies produced figures based on the number of particulates each tree can filter. They computed that 1 million trees 20 years old would filter 200 tons of pollutants from the air each day, bringing Los Angeles within 80 percent of the standards for particulates in the Clean Air Act. Based on that, they recommended planting 1 million trees, figuring it would take 20 years. However, there was neither the money nor the resources to implement the recommendation. When they contacted us we were presented with a rare opportunity."

Picture a million trees. Envision thousands of people working cooperatively to plant them all over one of the largest cities in the world. That is Andy Lipkis's dream. "If we can mobilize people to plant the trees, it will have benefits far beyond improving the air quality. Trees conserve energy by cooling buildings and cars and the air itself. Trees are also a source of food, and they provide a habitat for birds and animals. As I think of all the benefits, I know that planting trees is my life. Planting trees also brings people together cooperatively. When a person plants a tree, he or she is also planting a seed of caring in their heart."

Andy Lipkis's Tree People have built up tremendous public trust and confidence by responding to needs as they arise. For example, they have become a coordination point for volunteer efforts dealing with flood disasters. As with the tree planting, this was a matter of simply responding to a need.

"The floods hit Los Angeles right after we moved into our headquarters here. During the first storms a neighbor asked for help when the mud was coming down on his house. We got fifty other neighbors together, took out our tools, found sandbags and sand, and saved the house, at least for the time being. A city councilman heard what we had done, and when more big storms were expected, he asked if we would help organize volunteers. We started planning and when the big storms hit, we mobilized 800 volunteers in three days. We saved homes, and people realized if they needed help, they could count on the Tree People.

"All of these experiences have added to my belief in the power of commitment to community service. Some people are jealous of all the media coverage we have gotten and think we are successful simply because of that, but our success comes from a commitment to service.

"I think of myself as an environmentalist, but I am not really comfortable with the title because most environmentalists have defined themselves in terms of what they are against. I have always worked on a positive goal, like our current goal, 'Plant a million trees in the city before the 1984 Olympics.' Such a goal motivates people. The job will be done primarily with volunteers and with few paid staff. I have learned to depend upon the miracle of people working together. Programs, plans, estimates don't get trees planted; community will does. Planting a million trees is my largest goal, and in my mind I picture it done. Soon after I decided on our million-tree effort and before it was really announced, a nursery called to give us 100,000 trees they were about to destroy. When I asked, the army and air force said they would deliver them in one day, 50 trucks full of trees. Right after that someone at the school district decided that good relationships would emerge from black kids and white kids working together, and the district had the money to bus these children to where we were planting the trees.

"We wanted to start this project with a popular event. So I thought of a ten-kilometer race which would bring out people who would help us plant trees as the race was underway. The Los Angeles Police Department said we couldn't use Sepulveda Boulevard because there was no legislation to reimburse the police for overtime. The police said there are too many runs, anyway. Then by chance I found the Marina Freeway, which was five kilometers long, with a parking lot on one end for 5,000 cars. Perfect. But it crossed two city streets, which would have to be closed. The freeway belonged to the California Department of Transportation. They didn't want to lend it, but their stated policy is that they must turn it over if there is dramatic local support for the event. We went to the legislature with the proposal and finally, at the last minute, the legislature approved it. This project took everything I had for weeks, and I could not have done it without the personal support of my parents, my brothers, and my friends.

"When the police department balked at closing off the streets with officers, I reminded them of the disaster work we had done and that when a policeman was shot, we had fed 30 to 40 policemen on duty. The sergeant said we were right, that half of the men in his division had signed on to run the race. He went to the police commission and got the approval to close the street and staff it with officers. Three thousand people showed up for the run. Some runners planted trees along the way, and the event was simply beautiful. Each of the 3,000 participants got a tree to take home. The Tree People planted a grove of 70 trees along the freeway and watered it once. Now these drought-tolerant trees are 10 to 12 feet tall. Each year we go through the same hassle over the run, but each year someone wins the race, and each year more trees get planted.

"In all of the things we do, such as staging the race, helping in disasters, and planting trees, what we are really doing is educating people, and the media is helpful in this. When we give tours here in the park, make presentations to community groups and clubs, generate news stories, and plant trees, we are fulfilling our educational mission. By getting their hands in the ground, people learn about themselves and how they relate to everything else. Tree planting cuts across all ideologies, beliefs, and emotions."

Andy Lipkis thinks of himself as an environmentalist and an educator, but also as an artist. "An artist is someone who takes a portion of reality, puts a frame around it, and gives it to people so they see a truth and how they relate to it."

ELIZABETH TAPPE

A commitment to truth characterizes all of our models, but there are those who would argue that religious service is the pursuit of the highest truths.

In the center of Naugatuck, Connecticut, is a well-designed and restful green, with benches, statues, and historical markers shaded by old trees. On one corner of the green is St. Michael's Protestant Episcopal Church, a venerable red brick building more than 160 years old. The dark wooden pews, the cathedral vault, and the light from the stained glass windows give the interior an amber glow.

St. Michael's is one of the few Episcopal churches in Connecticut to have installed a female priest as assistant rector. She is Elizabeth

Tappe, and she has been at St. Michael's for more than two years, having previously held a ministry in the nearby city of Meriden.

Elizabeth Tappe is a comely woman in her late twenties with short light brown hair and a subdued manner. She wears a light biege skirt and a black long-sleeved blouse with a clerical collar. She was born in Hickory, North Carolina, went to St. Mary's College in Raleigh for two years, and then to the University of North Carolina at Chapel Hill.

"My parents were Episcopalians, devout Episcopalians, and I was too," said Mrs. Tappe. "In college I majored in religion. After graduation, I worked for a year as a medical secretary before deciding I wanted to become a college teacher of religion. In 1974 I entered Virginia Theological Seminary in Alexandria, matriculating in a two-year program leading to an advanced degree."

The Episcopal church, a branch of the Church of England, is one of the oldest religious denominations in the United States. In fact, in Virginia and New York, the Episcopal church was the established church, protected by law in colonial days. Principally because it is hierarchical, the Episcopal church did not move west with the pioneers as most other denominations did. There are a great many things a Baptist or Methodist pastor can do that in the Episcopal church only an Episcopal bishop can. For example, only a bishop can confirm communicants and ordain priests, and there were never many Episcopal bishops. Needless to say, it is a church with a great respect for tradition and for perpetuating that which has always been.

Women have been no strangers to religious rituals from the time of the Vestal Virgins of Rome through Jeanne d'Arc. There are women missionary runs in the Episcopal church, but none ever held ministerial office until 1970, when the General Convention decreed women could be ordained as deacons.

In 1974 3 bishops in Philadelphia ordained 11 women as Episcopal priests in a highly controversial ceremony. Many opposed the ordination of women on both canonical and Biblical grounds. St. Paul had argued that since Christ was a man only men should follow his ministry. But these proscriptions were not invincible dogma, and in 1976 the General Convention voted to permit the ordination of women as priests. Some bishops, priests, and dioceses still oppose the policy, making it difficult for female priests to obtain a ministry at a time when there are more applicants for parishes than there are parishes to go around.

Despite these obstacles Elizabeth Tappe decided she would become a priest. "I was led by God," she says. "There were no blinding flashes of light or mystical manifestations but a security and a confidence in me that wanted nothing else but wanted this passionately. The faculty at the seminary encouraged me. My parents supported the idea. The bishop assented. The only opposition I met came from my fellow seminarians.

"You have to understand that at this point no Episcopalian had listened to a woman preacher. There were no models to pattern myself after or to cite as effective priests. Moreover, many men simply do not consider women as equals. The feminist movement had a powerful influence on the country at large and strengthened my own determination. I was ordained by the bishop of North Carolina in 1978.

"Since then my own ministry has changed. At my first parish, I went to every meeting, volunteered for every program, was on call every minute of the day. It took me a year to realize I was neglecting one of my vows, which was to maintain a prayer life. A priest conducts not only communal but also solitary prayer. It is hard to conduct a ministry, but it is impossible if you do not pray by yourself every day. Sometimes all the work in the world will not bring about an effect. I have found that I am much more effective in my ministry as a counselor and a friend than I am at anything else. I am that because I am a counselor and a friend to myself.

"Insofar as women priests will change the church, they will bring to it a fuller dimension. If nothing else, women priests will teach us more about God who created a world of both men and women.

"When we talk about a happy marriage, we talk about two people who, because their biological and psychological differences complement each other, bring each other to a more complete fulfillment. I think that is what women priests will do for the church. They will bring a feminine quality and thus a greater completeness to it."

IAN McMILLAN

Working the land is deeply ingrained in this nation's tradition. Our final profile presents a farmer whose life is a model of respect for his environment.

The highway that cuts for more than 100 miles along the west side of the San Joaquin Valley in California seldom deviates, stretching as railroad rails and ties stretch toward the horizon. The fields to the east and west that provide much of the food for our tables lay bare, though cultivated. The rows are interrupted every so often by long irrigation pipes supported by dozens of wheels. Beyond the fields rest the mountains, which have the color and shape of slumbering lions.

The trip takes us northward into San Luis Obispo County and then west through the Temblor Range toward Shandon. Along the way the fields and rangelands now show only pitiful tufts of grass, flickering in the wind like votive candles. The pastures are dry and bare, overgrazed by beef cattle.

At Gillis Canyon Road, Ian McMillan meets us in his yellow pickup truck. McMillan is a 75-year-old farmer, with the weather-beaten face and wrinkled neck of a man constantly in the sun. He has blue eyes and wears a cowboy hat and boots; when he walks, his two interviewers have to run to keep up.

McMillan farms and grazes 1,360 acres on the south side of Gillis Canyon and 480 on the north side. Pointing north McMillan said, "That's the San Andreas Fault. Runs right along my land."

McMillan's barley has been harvested. His farm, in the foothills, curves and rolls upward from the road. Farmers here rotate their crops, grazing cattle on fallow fields sown with grass on alternate years. McMillan's fallow fields look rich. "I found you have to let a field lie fallow three years. Now I'm experimenting by letting some lie fallow for four years. I found that every stock cow needs 35 to 40 acres for grazing. That's why I keep my herd under 50 head."

Digging a small hole with the heel of his boot, he said, "This is the richest cereal land in the world. We do dry farming here with an average rainfall of ten inches. But a farmer has got to take care of his land or we can't survive. People are depleting these lands and depleting them fast. You can see it along the way you drove in."

"I was born in McMillan Canyon on my father's homestead, which he operated as a grain and cattle ranch. In some ways it was a hard life. He was in debt, but debt was common in those days. Actually, he handled very little money. He had a blacksmith's bill, a grocery bill, and a hardware bill each of which he paid once a year when he sold his wheat crop and his cattle.

"I finished grammar school and went to high school a few times until October came when farming started. In World War I, I gave up school because my two older brothers were in the service and we were short-handed at home. I don't want to say that I worked for my father because I enjoyed what I did, but we all put emphasis on workmanship and ability, and we all worked as a unit. I took my first job at 17, working on a harvester crew after our own harvest was over.

"My father bought some other property to provide for his sons, and this put him into debt. At the peak of his debt, here came the Depression, and he lost his place. Then too, we had a serious drought here in the early 1930s, and on top of everything, my father lost his health.

"My brothers and I scattered out, helping one another as much as we could. One brother bought his ranch in the 1930s with a veteran's loan, and he leased it to me cheaply. The small rent I paid amortized some of the debt. After a few years, he sold it to me. I moved up here in 1936 and bought the ranch in 1939.

"This came about because we brothers worked together. One of us worked this ranch, another that ranch, another one over there. We pooled our interests. It took little financing, although it took hard work. We bought an old secondhand tractor and went over to the San Joaquin Valley where we got 'tops' from the oil, the oil spilling directly from the well. You could actually burn it in a tractor. You could buy 'tops' for ten cents a gallon.

"We didn't make much money, but what we made we could use. So much cash in hand was a cow. Cash in the other hand was seed. This is the way we got along. I was able to get a wheat crop planted. The harvest came. There was money to work with then and I could buy more cattle.

"To buy this ranch today would cost $500,000. That's now the going price, though how anyone could recoup that investment I don't know. I make between $10,000 and $12,000 on my cattle. The others can't do much better. And if you borrow that half million, you'll pay 12 to 15 percent interest. I was able to make my ranch go without too many hands and with little money for which I paid 2 or 3 percent interest.

"When I started out, I had the opinion that this fantastically rich soil was an endless, inexhaustible resource. In its first cropping it was almost too rich to farm. We got volunteer crops here, the seeds that fall when we harvest grow another crop. The following year I thought that richness would be there forever.

"What changed my mind was the national problem of soil erosion. I was here when the Okies came through from Oklahoma and Texas and Arkansas. What had happened to them suddenly was happening more slowly on my own farm. After the first big crops, the yields started declining. We call it 'wearing out the land.' It started me thinking. I wanted an operation that assured a sustained yield.

"In World War II the agriculture experts were out, telling us how to plant every hill, every available acre. Well, in a year or two, I could see the soil washing down into the arroyos. That wouldn't do. The farm advisor came out and told us how to breed cattle so that there was more meat on them. It would do a farmer's heart good to see them so fat. But the trouble with the new breed was that the calves were so big, the cows couldn't birth them. So I bought some old longhorns and I don't have any more calving trouble.

"You'll also find a lot of experts telling you that growing juniper on your property is unorthodox and inefficient. It gets in the way of the cultivators. The government wants to get rid of junipers. The range experts take two tractors and hook a Libertyship anchor chain between them and wipe these juniper bushes out. But I let them grow. This country is turning into a desert. It is steadily losing plant life. I have read that the air is losing oxygen and that plants which convert carbon dioxide into oxygen are disappearing all over the world. I let the juniper grow because I like shade for my cattle. Instead of grouping densely under one or two juniper bushes, they can separate and get away from the heel fly. And the last reason, of course, is those bushes, scant though they be, are helping to hold that hill together and all the other hills. On slopes like that, every particle of plant life is reducing erosion.

"See, I own this spread. Some farmers lease their ranches from year to year. The lessee has to get in as big a crop and as high a turnover as possible—the devil with depletion. The owner wants the rent, and the lessee wants the profit. I don't see the concern for the land I think there should be. One day, though, folks will be amazed that we thought of land as chattel, that it belonged unto him who had it. I think the same folks will be amazed that we burned oil for fuel, because there are so many other things we can make from it.

"The major changes in farming came with the new technology—the new fertilizers, the new seeds that eliminated the necessity for concern over the land. Technology brings with it expensive machines. You have to use them all the time or lose money. The farm advisor says, 'The soil doesn't need to lie fallow.' They advise us to get rid of these plants called lupines, but lupines pump nitrogen into land that needs it. Point this out, and the experts say don't worry about lupines; there are far better ways of pumping nitrogen into the soil. But the new chemicals, the new stimulants, exhaust the land while giving the appearance of increased fertility.

"When I started out, I had a pen of hogs to supplement our income. We had chickens and Mrs. McMillan took the eggs and the poultry down to the grocery and put it toward our bill. And we made butter from our milk. Our income was marginal, but we got by and the kids even had piano lessons. When I consider my present income, I'm amazed at the amounts others say they must have for living.

"The land grant college system has a lot to do with the philosophy of farming. Through its extension service, it encourages maximum production. But the land resource of this semi-arid region can't sustain maximum production.

"I'm a small farmer. I don't want to be a part of a conglomerate with profit the driving motive. I have followed the plow and I know the difference in soil from one corner of this ranch to the other. I want to save the soil because I love it. And I love it for a good reason—because it lets me lead a satisfying and enriched life. Couldn't get along in business, on committees and on commissions. On a farm you're your own boss and make your own decisions. You don't get in arguments with the land.

"It's normal for a farmer to have big years and short years. You prepare for these. But now they have these disaster programs, and the local farmers run to the government for disaster money. Handouts is what they are. Handouts handicap the independent operator like me. Handouts go to those who overcrop their land, overgraze their ranges, pay no attention to anything but immediate maximum production and exploitation, those who thus are unprepared for the normal adversities that are part of farming.

"This hurts know-how. I grew up knowing that you don't run any more cattle than you can take care of in a short year. I voted to get the government off our backs. The 1970s have been prosperous. Show me an operator who cannot feed his cattle. Show me an operator who cannot buy seed. But this new administration isn't going to help get the government off our backs. Their new subsidy program operating under the name of 'Agriculture Stabilization and Conservation' provides for more of the same handouts."

McMillan led the authors from the house to his backyard to see his California quail. California quail is a game delicacy. The bird can fly for only short stretches, but it hops along the ground like the Road Runner of the animated cartoons. About four inches in height, three quail barely feed a hungry man. It is rapidly becoming extinct.

"Know why?" McMillan asked. "Because we tore the cover from the land. The quail can't hide from its predators, eagles and hawks."

McMillan is a farmer, perfectly integrated with his environment, in love with it. He is a man with a strong ethic, a land ethic. His ability to read the environment, to obey its dictates, and to change accordingly adds to the survival prospects of us all.

GOOD PLAYERS MAKE GREAT MUSIC

Isaac Stern, the violinist, was once asked why, when all musicians play the right notes in the right order, some make beautiful music and some do not. "The important thing is not the notes," he replied. "It is the interval *between* the notes." So it is with people. The important thing is the relationships among them and with their surroundings. These ten models for prosperity are virtuosos at playing the spaces—working cooperatively in their relationships with others and with their environments. By playing in concert with a larger whole, they have created beautiful music in their lives and in the lives of others.

6
Completing the Log

The value of a journey is what you learn along the way. As expressed by writer Ursula K. Le Guin, "It is good to have an end to journey towards; but it is the journey that matters, in the end."* We have charted the features of a preferred economic scenario as well as the life paths of ten models who have achieved prosperity and success in the broadest sense. We can complete the log by reviewing what we have learned.

The most important lessons have to do with the value of diversity, willingness to risk, openness to change, tolerance for uncertainty, commitment to a larger goal, and faith in a positive outcome. Additional lessons have to do with a cooperative approach and dedication to service, together with perseverance and hard work.

By matching up the personalities of the human models with the key features of the preferred economic scenario, we can see clearly what we need to do individually and collectively to produce the desired results.

---

*Ursula K. Le Guin, *The Left Hand of Darkness* (New York: Walker, 1969), p. 158.

DIVERSITY

Out of a thousand ventures many will fail, but some will work; it is those that work that count. By reviewing what works and why, we learn the lessons of survival and prosperity.

The first lesson concerns diversity. It takes a wide variety of people and paths in order to draw useful generalizations. Our group of models illustrates the point. Of the ten individuals profiled, each is unique; their life paths are strikingly different. No single model represents a mold into which others should fit, but, as we will see, the group as a whole provides some valuable pointers on what works for navigating in a sea of change.

PRODUCTIVITY AND RISK

Productivity improvement is the major feature of the preferred scenario. As we said in our example of the Robinson Crusoe island economy, productivity is based on *investment* (to expand capital goods and improve their efficiency) and *learning* (to increase the proficiency of labor). In the preferred scenario the real rate of private investment is increased by 3.5 percent per year. By the year 2000 investment grows from 14 percent of GNP to 16 percent. Government spending is reduced from the current 23 percent of GNP to 20 percent. To get these results personal income taxes will have to be cut from 25 percent in 1980 to 11 percent by 1990 and corporate taxes cut to 20 percent from the present 46 percent. The tax laws must also be modified to provide individuals and companies with incentives for saving and investing the money the government is no longer taking from them.

For the individual, saving and investing means sacrifice and accepting risks. In the words of Charles Peters, "The key to a more vital economy is to forget failure, forget the fear that invests it. We need civil servants and presidents, economists and reporters who are adventurous and willing to take risks to bring about beneficial ends."

Peters practices what he preaches. "I was perfectly well aware that the magazine business was a more hazardous living than managing a restaurant. But optimistically I thought the *Monthly* would catch on faster than it did. I had to mortgage and remortgage the house to keep the magazine going."

Jim Roseboro expresses the needed attitude toward investment and risk succinctly: "Capital investment is a risk, but what isn't?" Though he works for a larger organization than does Jim Roseboro, Bill Gould conveys this attitude in another way. Speaking of the decision to commit to alternative and renewable energy sources, Gould says, "What we really gave up was comfort, and I have given up comfort many times in the past."

Doing without comfort and security is not limited to the business world. Labor leader Robert Georgine says, "If you lose an election, it's back to the tools.... There've been a lot of changes in my union, but that hasn't changed. You don't get kicked upstairs when you lose an election."

Each of the models is willing to accept risks and has a deep-seated faith that things will work out. One either has faith or does not. Picture a man walking down the sidewalk saying to himself, "Fifty-six years and not one crack." Faith is being willing to step on some cracks from time to time. You cannot expect to win every time, but you can feel that if you stay in the game you will come out alright.

OPENNESS TO CHANGE

To take risks you must be open to accept change. Change, after all, is what makes things risky. It was Benjamin Franklin who said, "In this world nothing is certain but death and taxes." Sage old Ben could have added change to his list. In the natural universe and especially in the affairs of humanity, nothing is static; everything is changing, every minute. The Greek philosopher Heraclitus wrote in 500 B.C., "Nothing is permanent except change." Some people recognize and accept this reality; others try to deny and resist it. In *Gone With the Wind*, Margaret Mitchell's epic novel about the passing of the old South, she expresses this bit of philosophy, "Life's under no obligation to give us what we expect. We take what we get and are thankful it's no worse than it is."*

---

*Margaret Mitchell, *Gone With the Wind* (New York: Macmillan, 1936), p. 926.

Technological and social change now accelerates faster than at any other period in history. Living through such change is undeniably stressful and frustrating. Just when you figure out an answer to a big question, another big question arises. Sometimes it seems that solutions lead only to new problems.

The price of the great benefits and opportunities of the information age is constant change, which means uncertainty, risk, and fear. The illusion that certainty is desirable is alluring. But the price of certainty would be much higher than the risks and fear of uncertainty. The price of knowing the future and having solutions we are certain will work is the loss of freedom to choose. Loren Eiseley described *The Unexpected Universe* in the following manner:

> Science is a solver of problems, but it is dealing with the limitless, just as, in a cruder way, were the Romans. Solutions to problems create problems; their solutions, in turn, multiply into additional problems that escape out of scientific hands like noxious insects into the interstices of the social fabric. The rate of growth is geometric, and the vibrations set up can even now be detected in our institutions. This is what the Scottish biologist D'Arcy Thompson called the evolution of contingency. It is no longer represented by the long, slow turn of world time as the geologist has known it. Contingency has escaped into human hands and flickers unseen behind every whirl of our machines, every pronouncement of political policy.*

Do our models offer any guidance for dealing with change and uncertainty? Yes. Each of their lives was changed by unanticipated events in the world around them. But rather than resisting the unexpected, they turned it to advantage. Jack Horton had decided to become a small town lawyer when World War II intervened. He wound up at Standard Oil, *expecting* to be drafted, but was not. He was given instead an exceptional opportunity to acquire experience while still quite young. Then he decided to stay with a local utility company in place of Standard Oil because he did not want to move his home. Almost immediately he was sent to Canada. It was certainly not what Horton had in mind, but he made the most of it; in fact, it led directly to the top position at Southern California Edison.

---

*Loren Eiseley, *The Unexpected Universe* (New York: Harcourt, Brace & World, 1969), pp. 43–44.

His openness to change and willingness to experiment carried over into Horton's management style. In his words, "I've learned the importance of creating an atmosphere of openness in which the officers and department heads are free to communicate without fear of harassment if they recommend something that their boss doesn't like." Concerning SCE's investment in research and development, he says, "I always insisted to our vice-presidents that when someone presents a proposal you think is crazy, you'd better take a long and careful look at it. It is important to find out whether he's crazy or you're crazy."

Norm King talks about the value of change and the value of diversity in the same breath. Speaking of his city of Palm Springs, he says, "Every city has its own unique mix of social, physical, and economic conditions. That is what makes city management so vital. If you think about it, that is the strength of this country, along with the fact that it is always changing." King thinks of change as something that creates strength.

It is the fear of change that paralyzes, not change itself. Life is not simple or easy, and diversity and change are essential to survival. In the information economy the explosion of new companies and entrepreneurial ventures assures a vital and dynamic economy in the next two decades. As has been said, "The best way to have a good idea is to have a lot of ideas."

Some of our models have even sought to make change a central goal in their lives. Elizabeth Tappe chose to go where no woman had gone before. As she says, "You have to understand that at this point, no Episcopalian had listened to a woman preacher. There were no models to pattern myself after or to cite as effective priests. Moreover, many men simply do not consider women as equals."

COMMITMENT TO A LARGER GOAL

Jim Roseboro made personal changes with larger social change in mind. For him, changing from a college teaching job and going into his own business was a means, not an end. In his words, "I knew that teaching and research were not to be my life's only work. I had a growing sense of wanting to contribute to social change. My ultimate goal was to go into my own business in order to become financially independent and then attempt to influence events. I wanted to contribute more to the changing social scene."

Norm King's larger vision is described in terms of a "systems view." He thinks of a city as a "complex interconnected organism." In his view, "We need to look at a total system to manage demand as well as supply of public services." Seeing from a systems perspective gives one a sense of the interconnectedness of things. It requires a broader view and a concern for the longer-term effects of current decisions. King approaches his city budgets that way. "In this economic climate there is a tendency to take a short-term view by deferring maintenance expenditures. I urged the council not to mortgage the future in this way. I am gratified that both in Claremont and Palm Springs the city councils took the difficult step of cutting programs rather than deferring maintenance. They realized that deferring maintenance is not a savings; the costs are simply shifted to future taxpayers."

A larger vision and goal is the primary motivating force for Andy Lipkis. Planting trees and the other activities of the Tree People are a means to a larger end. "In all of the things we do, such as staging the race, helping in disasters, and planting trees, what we are really doing is educating people, and the media is helpful in this. When we give tours here in the park, make presentations to community groups and clubs, generate news stories, and plant trees, we are fulfilling our educational mission. By getting their hands in the ground, people learn about themselves and how they relate to everything else. Tree planting cuts across all ideologies, beliefs, and emotions." Andy learned this lesson at an early age. Describing his experience at a summer camp while in high school, he says, "Those who worked in the project learned a vital truth—people will identify with a positive solution to a problem, and they will work hard for it. This kind of work creates energy and excitement; so you don't get tired." In summing up his 28 years of experience and the success of the Tree People, he shares: "All of these experiences have added to my belief in the power of commitment to community service. Some people are jealous of all the media coverage we have gotten and think we are successful simply because of it, but our success comes from a commitment to service."

In her pursuit of change and services, Elizabeth Tappe was motivated by the largest purpose of all, the service of God.

DEDICATION TO COMMUNITY AND SERVICE

Commitment to a larger goal and working in service to community are crucial aspects of our preferred path to national prosperity. All of our models share that commitment, but to Andy Lipkis they are the elements of a personal identity. "I think of myself as an environmentalist, but I am not really comfortable with the title because most environmentalists have defined themselves in terms of what they are against. I have always worked on a positive goal, like our current goal, to plant a million trees in the city before the 1984 Olympics. Such a goal motivates people. The job will be done primarily with volunteers and with few paid staff. I have learned to depend upon the miracle of people working together. Programs, plans, estimates don't get trees planted; community will does."

Interestingly enough, the professional managers at the Southern California Edison Company hold the same strong commitment to community service as Andy Lipkis. When Bill Gould speaks about the pressures upon and opposition to utility companies over the last decade, he says, "We made a conscious decision that we would not abandon our commitment to serve the public, that we would discharge our responsibility to the public trust, that somehow we would find a way to serve."

COOPERATION

To Gould, as for Jack Horton, cooperation is the means for fulfilling a commitment to service. In fact, cooperation is consistently sought by all of our models. Gould set down his view of the specific meaning of cooperation in the article he wrote for the *General Electric Forum* magazine. Writing as a vice-president for engineering in the mid-1960s he said, "Because governmental agencies and the utilities alike are servants of the same ultimate customers, the general public, we must cooperate to the best ultimate interest of that public. In my opinion, this demands a recognition by each of the responsible roles of the other. It demands full and honest communication of intent and objective, and a thorough discussion of the social problems with which we are mutually concerned, together with a thorough evaluation of alternate solutions to them."

Robert Georgine has the same orientation to cooperation in the context of labor-management relations. Faced with continuously changing construction technology, Georgine and his union members have repeatedly adjusted their work rules. "The contractors argued why did they have to install windows on the thirteenth floor when on the twenty-second the men were working without walls. So we dispensed with the requirement." "The architects and the engineers came up with new ways of hanging ceilings and new alloys; so the contractors went to the union for relief. And the members decided that it was not the union's responsibilty to determine safety nor was it equipped to do so. They were there to work, not to police quality."

"Men who worked on the grids of a skeleton skyscraper got more money because their work was dangerous. Management objected to these pay differentials. We agreed with management. No worker anywhere for any reason should work in peril. We gave up the differentials, and management made the grid of the skeleton safe.

"These are some of the technical reasons we change. But we change, too, because there are areas where management and labor have much in common."

Finding ways to work cooperatively in the field of labor-management relations is a challenge for both sides. But one even greater test of the ability to work cooperatively is to do it in the face of discrimination and prejudice. In this regard Josie Bain is an exemplary model. When she went to apply for a job at the board of education, she was told, "You can't take the exam, you don't have the needed background, and furthermore we don't have any openings for you." Josie did not fight the situation, she just did not accept it, and she worked her way around it.

WORK AND PERSEVERANCE

Willingness to work combined with perseverance and cooperation are the trademarks of Josie Bain's success from grade school to membership on the state board of education. As she says, "I was willing to work hard, staying with a given task until it was completed. Lastly, I had hopes, and hope is the beginning of movement.

Hope gives one the will and determination to use all available resources, including people, to achieve a given level of service."

Here is the pattern found in all of the models for survival and prosperity: the will to work and to succeed through cooperation; hope coupled with a belief in a positive outcome; and a commitment to service. Positive attitude coupled with action gets results, and results are what count. For many people, after all is said and done, there is a lot more said than done. Our models are people who, once they found something out, acted on it and got results.

Each individual profiled comes from a different environment, which means that their similar traits have found diverse expression. Ian McMillan is perfectly adapted to the land, and it is with the land that he has learned to work and cooperate. When McMillan thinks of cooperation, it is in a very different context from that of Jose Bain and the other people profiled. For Ian McMillan cooperation with the land is an affair of the heart. "I want to save the soil because I love it. And I love it for a good reason—because it lets me lead a satisfying and enriched life. I couldn't get along in business, on committees and on commissions. On a farm you're your own boss and make your own decisions. You don't get in arguments with the land." But McMillan's focus on the elemental factor of earth is not as unique as it may seem at first. Some basic truths span time and space, from antiquity to the sophisticated world of a board chairman. Bill Gould wrote in 1967, "Among the elementary environmental factors identified by the ancient Greeks were earth, air, and water. It is around these elements of our ecology that the energy-producing industry faces its greatest challenges."

CHOICE OVER CHANCE

The sum total of individual decisions will determine the success of the nation on its collective pathway to prosperity. Thus there is value in studying the attitudes, beliefs, and choices of people who have dealt successfully with major changes and in so doing added to the survival and prosperity of the whole.

The economic and energy future will be strongly influenced by human perceptions, beliefs, and attitudes working through the powerful social force of the "self-fulfilling prophecy." To illustrate how this dynamic works, consider the problems of the marriage matchmaker in traditional societies. Starting with the interests and preferences of two sets of parents, the matchmaker proposes a union sure to earn mutual gratitude and a handsome fee if consummated. The scheme is sometimes frustrated however by the fact that the two young people may have no interest whatsoever in each other. This is where matchmakers earn their professional standing because they are masters of the "self-fulfilling prophesy." The matchmaker says to young David, "Have you noticed how Sara looks at you?" To Sara he says, "David thinks you are wonderful. He can't keep his eyes off of you." Until that time David and Sara have barely noticed each other. But now, when they next meet, they look to see if the other is looking. Indeed, each is looking—and things begin to happen.

We can see in this illustration a profound difference between the way things work in the social world and the way they work in the physical world. In the latter a statement that a cubic foot of natural gas will produce 2,000 Btus, twice the known yield, will in no way influence an experiment designed to check the facts. In the human world, however, the matchmaker's statements, "David is interested in you, Sara," and "Sara is interested in you, David," while not true when made, may become true if they are believed by Sara and David. In human relations (which includes economics) beliefs, attitudes, and intentions can produce outcomes. The preferred path to prosperity is not only possible, it is probable, if we intend it, choose it, and believe in it. On the other hand, if we believe that growth and prosperity are beyond our grasp, we will help bring on a future of stagnation. By holding a vision of success in achieving our fullest national potential, we enhance the possibility of new solutions and unexpected options. The decision is a matter of personal choice made by the individual and projected into the society at large.

Over the past two decades, the United States has been guided by the self-fulfilling prophecies of economic impotence, energy dependence, and the inevitability of conflict resulting in a nuclear war. We have looked for and found limits in place of opportunities. This book has pointed out the personal and collective choices of a future characterized by prosperity and well-being. It has looked back into the lives of real people to see how success was achieved in different contexts by individuals who share some qualities that work. It looked forward through the experiences of some imaginary characters to see how the preferred path would influence and be influenced by the choices of individuals over the next 20 years. It remains for real people to believe in and choose their own avenues to prosperity.

If public policy choices made in the United States were consistent with those laid out in the preferred scenario and the composite character of the models presented, it would matter little what happened to world oil prices and other chance factors outside our control. Even assuming bad luck in the form of constantly rising oil prices, GNP would grow by 3 percent per year and afford a climate of prosperity through the year 2000. A combination of coal, nuclear, synfuels, and solar power would round out the energy picture and hold the consumption of oil at the 1978 level. By the year 2000 imports would provide only 30 percent of total U.S. oil consumption and 6 percent of total energy use. Minimizing our dependence on external sources of energy would reduce world competition for scarce energy supplies and lessen the economic and political pressures fueling the arms race. The continuing worldwide shift to an information/service-based economy will have a similar positive effect. Diversity in sources of energy and economic wealth promotes survival and prosperity. That pathway to prosperity is worth investing in and working for.

There are myriad opportunities in this country. Our system offers the widest range of freedom available to any people in the world. It gives individuals the opportunity to be what they can be and institutions the chance to change and renew. But there are no guarantees. Individuals and institutions can choose to stay dynamic and vital or to become fixed in habit and routine. One old idea inherited from the Great Depression is that of turning to government for answers to problems. By demanding too much from our political system, we compromise the society's ability to accept and adapt to change.

Government does not possess the keys to success and survival. Those ingredients are, first, an adequate base of energy-bearing and other raw materials; second, an advanced, highly developed technology and industry including an unequalled modern agricultural production system; third, and most important, an educated, motivated, and trainable population, one that embraces the character traits of our ten models.

The necessary ingredients are available, but every movement and every gain carries a cost. We learn from experience: from families, friends, and workmates. The meaning of life cannot be found in the dictionary. We learn and relearn by working and keeping commitments, by facing crises, and by suffering. Even change for the better can be painful. But there is great joy and satisfaction in learning. The spirit grows in depth and enthusiasm.

The second law of thermodynamics teaches us that the physical universe is ruled by entropy; things always decay. But entropy is not something to regret; indeed, it is what keeps life interesting and meaningful. Without decay of the old, there would be no renewal. An entropy-free system would require little or no effort. Struggle and effort are the source of satisfaction in life. Thus entropy is a given and an advantage; everything depends on how one relates to it. Life is a process of responding and relating—to things, people, and larger realities such as entropy. The things we desire or seek to avoid are not objects but relationships. No one wants a chair, or an orange, or a pearl for its own sake. The owner wants to sit in it, eat it, wear it, admire it, give it, or merely possess it—in one way or another to have some relation to it. Relations with people are far more complex, dynamic, and interesting, involving deeper feelings.

All of our goals and activities are about establishing, maintaining, or changing relationships, and of all the possible ways to relate cooperation is the most challenging and rewarding. That is the central guidepost leading to *Pathways to Prosperity*.

Bibliography

American Petroleum Institute. *Two Energy Futures: A National Choice for the 80s.* Washington, D.C.: API, 1980.

Choate, Pat. *As Time Goes By: The Costs and Consequences of Delay.* Columbus, Ohio: Academy for Contemporary Problems, 1980.

Cooper, Ronald L. "The Energy-Economy Connection: 1974-1979 and Beyond." *Business Economics*, September 1980, pp. 5-11.

Council on Environmental Quality and the Department of State. *The Global 2000 Report to the President.* Washington, D.C.: Government Printing Office, 1980.

Denison, Edward F. *Accounting for Slower Economic Growth: The United States in the 1970s.* Washington, D.C.: Brookings Institution, 1979.

Dogramaci, Ali, ed. *Productivity Analysis: A Range of Perspectives.* Boston: Martinus Nijhoff, 1981.

Dumas, Lloyd J., ed. *The Political Economy of Arms Reduction: Reversing Economic Decay.* Boulder, Colo.: Westview Press, 1982.

Easterlin, Richard Ainley. *Birth and Fortune: The Impact of Numbers on Personal Welfare.* New York: Basic Books, 1980.

Edison Electric Institute. *Economic Growth in the Future: The Growth Debate in National and Global Perspective.* New York: McGraw-Hill, 1976.

Eiseley, Loren. *The Unexpected Universe.* New York: Harcourt, Brace & World, 1969.

Employment Research Associates. *The Empty Pork Barrel.* Lansing, Mich.: ERA, 1982.

Etzioni, Amitai. "Choose We Must." In *The Individual and the Future of Organizations.* Franklin Foundation Lecture Series, vol. 9, edited by Carl A.

Bramlette, Jr. and Michael H. Mescon, pp. 25-39. Atlanta: Business Publishing Division, College of Business Administration, Georgia State University, 1980.

Evans, Christopher. *The Micro Millennium.* New York: Washington Square Press, 1981.

Fabricant, Solomon. *The Economic Growth of the United States: Perspective and Prospect.* Washington, D.C.: National Planning Association, 1979.

Feldstein, Martin, ed. *The Economy in Transition.* Chicago: University of Chicago Press, 1980.

Frankl, Viktor E. *Man's Search for Meaning: An Introduction to Logotherapy.* New York: Simon & Schuster, 1963.

Ginzberg, Eli, and George J. Vojta. "The Service Sector of the U.S. Economy." *Scientific American*, March 1981, pp. 48-55.

Hibbing, John R. "Voluntary Retirement From the U.S. House: The Costs of Congressional Service." *Legislative Studies Quarterly* (February 1982).

Hyman, Edward J. *Attitudes Toward Economic Growth and the Environment.* Berkeley: Center for Social Research, 1980.

The Independent Commission on Disarmament and Security Issues. *Common Security: A Blueprint for Survival.* New York: Simon & Schuster, 1982.

International Business Network. "Record Defense Budgets Harmful to Small Business: Expert Urges Reagan to Consider New Russian Offer." *Position Paper.* Santa Monica, Calif., September 16, 1982.

Kendrick, John W. *Understanding Productivity: An Introduction to the Dynamics of Productivity Change.* Policy Studies in Employment and Welfare, no. 31. Baltimore: Johns Hopkins University Press, 1977.

Kipling, Rudyard. Prelude to "Departmental Duties." *Rudyard Kipling Verse: The Definitive Edition*, 1885.

Le Guin, Ursula K. *The Left Hand of Darkness.* New York: Walker, 1969.

Lerner, Barbara. "American Education: How Are We Doing?" *The Public Interest*, Fall 1982.

Lynn, Richard. Article in *Nature*, May 20, 1982, as reported in the *Washington Post*, June 13, 1982, p. A14.

Mitchell, Margaret. *Gone With the Wind.* New York: Macmillan, ©1936, renewed 1964 and 1966.

Murray, Charles A. "The Two Wars Against Poverty: Economic Growth and the Great Society." *The Public Interest*, Fall 1982.

Naisbitt, John. *Megatrends: Ten New Directions Transforming Our Lives.* New York: Warner Books, 1982.

Peck, M. Scott. *The Road Less Traveled.* New York: Simon & Schuster, 1978.

Perloff, Harvey, ed. *The Future of the United States Government—Toward the Year 2000.* New York: George Braziller, 1971.

Rathbun, Harry J. *Creative Initiative: Guide to Fulfillment.* Palo Alto, Calif.: Creative Initiative Foundation, 1976.

Report of a Special Task Force to the Secretary of Health, Education and Welfare. *Work in America.* Cambridge, Mass.: MIT Press, 1972.

"Revitalizing the U.S. Economy." *Business Week*, June 30, 1980, pp. 56–142.

Saffady, William. *The Automated Office: An Introduction to the Technology.* Silver Spring, Md.: National Micrographics Association, 1981.

Schell, Jonathan. *The Fate of the Earth.* New York: Alfred A. Knopf, 1982.

Servan-Schreiber, Jean-Jacques. *The World Challenge.* New York: Simon & Schuster, 1981.

Sivard, Ruth L. *World Military and Social Expenditures 1982.* Leesburg, Va.: World Priorities, 1982.

Spolin, Viola. *Improvisation for the Threatre.* Evanston, Ill.: Northwestern University Press, 1963.

Stobaugh, Robert, and Daniel Yergim, eds. *Energy Future. Report of the Energy Project at the Harvard Business School.* New York: Random House, 1979.

Technology Forecasts. Newsletter, Los Angeles, October 1981 and June 1982.

Thompson, William F., Jerome J. Karaganis, and Kenneth D. Wilson. *Choice over Chance: Economic and Energy Options for the Future.* New York: Praeger, 1981.

Turner, Stansfield. "Is the U.S. Pinning False Hopes on the MX System?" *Los Angeles Times*, September 20, 1981, pt. 5, p. 3.

U.S., Congress, Joint Economic Committee. *The Joint Economic Report.* Annual reports to Congress on the annual *Economic Report of the President* for 1979-81. Washington, D.C.: Government Printing Office, 1979-81.

U.S., Department of Energy, Assistant Secretary for Policy and Evaluation. *Reducing U.S. Oil Vulnerability: Energy Policies for the 1980s.* Report to the secretary of energy. Washington, D.C.: Government Printing Office, 1980.

U.S., President's Commission for a National Agenda for the Eighties, Panel on American Economy: Employment, Productivity, and Inflation. *The American Economy: Employment, Productivity, and Inflation in the Eighties.* Washington, D.C.: Government Printing Office, 1980.

Wilson, Kenneth D., ed. *Prospects for Growth: Changing Expectations for the Future.* New York: Praeger, 1977.

Index

academic proficiency, testing of, 107
acid rain, 13
air flow, 116
antiballistic missile system, 74
Arab oil embargo, 10
Arab sea, 12
arms control, public opinion on, 73
arms race, 71; and economic exhaustion, 18; and economic growth, 17
army policy, revelations of, 111
auto industry, 95

Bain, J., 103–109; early education, 103–104; motivation, 106; as role model, 105
birth rate, 27
bracket creep, 61
Brezhnev, L., 12
business: and computers, 51; and government, 6; and risks, 76
business investment, interest rate, 61
business property taxes, 100
business regulations, 66
buying power, 33

cable television, 52
Callaghan, D., 55
capital investment, 9
Capra, J., 72
cattle breeding, 123
censorship, 110
cereal land, 121
Choice over Chance: Economic and Energy Options for the Future, 22–24
citizens, and local government, 97
city government, 97; citizens attitude, 98; council meetings, 99; and courts, 98; and federal government, 100; financial planning, 100; maintenance expenditures, 100; pollution control, 99; public services, 132; safety measures, 99; sanitation department, 101; service systems, 101; social services, 99; and state, 100; zoning laws, 98

city management, 102
city managers, 96, 97
city projects, 97
civil rights movement, 89
Clean Air Act, 36, 116
climate changes, 25
coal, 11, 69; burning, 69; prices, 37
coal prices, increase in, 37
collective bargaining, 79, 92
college education and tax exemption, 42
communication technology, 50; and energy use, 51
community, services to, 117, 133
campaign manager, 110
Computer revolution, 54
Computers: and education, 53; and electricity use, 52; and environment, 90; and genetic experiments, 91; and national productivity, 54; and office work, 53; and youth, 54
Comte, A., 2
conservation organization, 113
Continental Shelf, 68
corporate leadership, 84
corporate taxes, 42
cooperation, 80
cooperative work, 116
crop lands, 12
crop yield, 123
Crusoe, R., 31, 32
curricula, reorienting, 57–59

death rate, 27
decisiveness, 84
developing countries, 10; energy needs, 10
disaster programs, 124
discrimination, 134
drought, 122
dry farming, 121

econometrics, 23
economic forecasting, 2, 21; energy choices, 68; energy problems, 36–38; immigration effect, 27; and labor force, 28;

model characters, 39-47; modeling, 22; and population trends, 27; and working hours, 29
economic growth, 8; and energy use, 15
economic model, 23; assumptions, 24; and demography, 24; and fiscal policy, 25; and labor force factor, 25; and productivity factor, 25; and world energy, 25
economic policy: choices, 49-74; recommendations, 49
economic problems, 49
economic productivity, 9
economic stability, 3
economic success, and intelligence, 58
economy, 4, 7; transition period, 49, 50
education: corporate donations, 59; government spending in, 58
education system, and economy, 9
Eiseley, L., 130
electric utilities: and changing environment, 78; energy audit, 78; environmental concern, 77; future planning, 76; generating capacity, 83; investments in, 83; load growth, 77; marketing, 77; oil consumption, 77; and oil prices, 77; partnerships, 86; rate increase, 77; research and development, 78; and review of nuclear licensing, 70
electricity, conservation of, 78
employers, and labor unions, 93
energy conservation, 11
energy industry, construction in, 94
energy management, 51
energy policy, 67
energy problems, 36
energy self-sufficiency, 67
energy sources, 10-12; geothermal, 85; hydroelectric, 85; oil, 10; renewable, 11, 85; soil, 11; water, 11, 12
entropy, 15-16
environment: adaptation to, 87; capital investment for, 35; human exploitation, 13-14; industrial effect on, 13
environmental legislation, people's influence on, 115
environmental protection, 44; cost of, 13, 36; and private organizations, 67
Environmental Protection Agency, 66
environmentalists, 117
Episcopal church, 119
Evans, C., 51

factory workers, 29
failure, fear of, 112
farmers, 120; disaster programs and, 124; and government, 124, 125
farming: new fertilizers, 123; technology, 123
federal agencies, working of, 111
federal aid, cutbacks in, 62
federal budget, balancing of, 63
federal minimum wage, 66
Federal Reserve Board, 62
feminist movement, 120
financial independence, 90
flood disasters, 116
food: distribution of, 12; prices, 12; production of, 11, 12; transportation of, 12
forest conservation, 115

genetic engineering, 14
genetic pool, 14
Georgine, R., 91-95
GI Bill, 106
Global 2000 Report to the President, The, 10
GNP, *see* gross national product
goals: commitment to, 127; focusing on, 3-5; positive, 117
Gould, W. R., 81-87; corporate leadership, 84; decisiveness, 84
government: anthropological aspects, 112; and censorship, 110; evaluation, 111; investment policies, 60; job programs, 56; process of, 109; and publicity, 110
government deficits, 7
government money, and local communities, 95
government regulations, 65-67
government spending, 35; control of, 61; reduction of, 62; and Vietnam war, 61
government workers, 62
greenhouse effect, 13
gross national product (GNP), 64; growth of, 26; investments and, 34; as measurement of economic performance, 25-26

heterogenous society, 3
home computer industry, 88
home computers, 53
hope, 108
Horton, J., 76; early life, 79; personal success, 81
housing, 8, 9; and wildlife, 14
human relations, 136

humanity, and environment, 85
hydroelectric power, 85, 86

immigration, 27-28
income, personal, 26
income tax: corporate, 61; reduction of, 36
individual responsibility v. government regulation, 65-67
industrial revolution, 29
industrial robots, 50
inflation, 8; and government spending, 61
information economy, 50; diversity, 52; educational requirements, 57; and labor productivity, 55; and microprocessors, 51; and political parties, 50; private sector, 58; and unemployment, 56; and work, 56; workers training, 57
information society: effect on education, 52; and financial market, 54
information workers, 50
international trade, 31
interstate highways, 9
investment, 34, 42, 47; and GNP, 34; policy choices, 60; private, 35; productive, 87; and savings, 34; tax credit, 36
IQ scores, 58

job satisfaction, and productivity, 30
junipers, 123

King, Norman, 96-102; early life, 96, 97

labor environment, changes in, 95
labor leaders, 91
labor management relations, 134
labor productivity, 9, 32; growth, 55
labor progress, 93
labor unions, 57; and contractors, 94; elections, 92; lobbying, 93; membership, 93; and nuclear energy, 95; and technology, 94
landfills, 101
land grant college system, 124
leadership, 18; prosperity goals and, 18
LeGuin, U. K., 127
Lerner, B., 58
life, quality of, 47
life expectancy, 27
Lipkis, A., 113-118
local government, and Proposition 13, 100, 101

Los Angeles: air pollution, 116; floods, 116; police department, 117
lupines, 124
Lynn, R., 58

Madison, J., 65
"make-it-happen" committee, 86
management, and labor, 92
manufacturing industries, and labor unions, 57
McMillan, I., 120-125; early life, 121
microprocessors, 51
military contractors, 33
military spending: inflationary effect on, 72; reduction in, 71; and small business, 72; and unemployment, 71
model characters: opportunities, 39; policy choices, 39; and prosperous life, 45; and risk, 40; saving and investment, 40; and tax cut, 40
moral commitment, 90
Mosher, C. A., 18
motivation, 106, 107
Moynihan, P., 66
Murray, C., 26

national debt, reduction of, 65
national decisions, 1
national defense, 54
national prosperity: and cooperation, 133; commitment to goals, 133; people's choices, 135; willingness to work, 134-135
national security, 4
natural gas, 38, 68; price deregulation, 68
navy contractors, 33
Neal, R. H., 89
nuclear energy, risks of, 69
nuclear fuel, 11
nuclear reactors, 38; accidents, 70; as electric generators, 38
nuclear testing, atmospheric, 89
nuclear war, 16-18; economic cost, 71; preparation for, 17; survivors of, 17; threat of, 70
nuclear weapons, 17

occupations, 57
office productivity, and national economy, 56
oil consumption, 10
oil embargo, 3, 67

146 / PATHWAYS TO PROSPERITY

oil prices, 10, 37; increase in, 37
oil production, in U.S., 10
oil resources, 37, 68; recovery techniques, 68
oil supplies, 10
on-the-job training, 59, 66
opium, 17

pastures, 121
Peace Corps, 110; evaluative reports, 111
Peking, and water level, 12
pension plans, 31
personal change, 131
personal identity, and commitment to goals, 133
Peters, C., Jr., 109-113
physical laws, society and, 15
poverty, 26
prejudice, 106
preventive medicine, 102
priest, female, 118
printing press, invention of, 53
private firms, 64
private investment, 35; rate, 128; and risks, 128
productive investment, 87
productivity, 8, 31-36; and economic growth, 31; and government spending, 35; growth rate, 32, 54; improved factors for, 32; and inflation, 9, 31; and international trade, 31; and new investments, 33, 34
productivity improvement, 9, 32, 59, 128
property taxes, 100
Proposition 13, 100, 101
prosperity: and economic growth, 1; and environment, 13; future planning, 1-6, 21-47; government role, 59; goals, 21-47; and intelligence, 16; as national goal, 3; and natural resources, 1; and nuclear war, 16-18; and public works, 64
prosperity goals, 21-47; energy shortage and, 10; environmental hazards, 13; hazards to, 7-19; and leadership, 18; nuclear war hazards, 16; planning for, 21
prosperity models, 75-125; adaptation, 76; diversity, 128; flexibility, 79; leadership qualities, 84; response to change, 75; and risks, 129; and uncertainty, 130
Protestant work ethic, 29
public consensus, 19

public works: deterioration, 63; governmental spending, 64; maintenance cost, 64
publicity, 110
publishers, 109

quails, 125

racial discrimination, 107
radiation fallout, 89
radiation hazards, 89
rain forests, 14
ranch leasing, 123
recession, 63, 92
religion, 119
religious service, 118
research and development, 60
retirement age, 30
retirement income, inadequacy of, 31
riots, effect on schools, 107
risks, 2, 3, 112, 113; willingness, 127
role model, 105
Roseboro, J. A., 88-91; early life, 88, 89

Saffady, W., 55
San Andreas Fault, 12
savings: interest rate, 61; policy choices, 60
Schell, J., 74
school administration, 106
school principals, training program, 106
school system: art programs, 107; and community, 107
school teachers: substitute, 105; training of, 107; transfers, 106
self-fulfilling prophecy, 135-136
self-worth, personal, 108
skyscrapers, 94
small businesses, 72, 73, 88
smog, 113
social change, 91, 130
social security, 31
social welfare, 62
society, and physical laws, 15
soil erosion, 123
soil richness, 122
solar collectors, 37
solar energy, 37, 69
Southern California Edison Co. (SCE), 76-87
Soviet Union, food shortages in, 12
space program, 59
Spolin, V., 16
sprinkler systems, 101

Steadman, C. W., 65
steel industry, 95
strikes, 92
suburban transit systems, 42
substitute teacher, 105
success, personal, 81
survival, and prosperity, 5, 128
synfuel, *see* synthetic fuel
synthetic fuel, 37; cost of, 69; future cost, 37

Tappe, E., 118–120; early life, 119; prayers, 120
teaching machines, 52
teaching techniques, 107
technological change, 130
thermodynamics, laws of, 15
Third World, deforestation, 14
trade imbalance, 7
tree planting, 113, 114, 115; and air pollution, 116
Tree People, 113, 118
trees: and energy conservation, 116; as food source, 116; and wildlife, 116
Turner, S., 73

uncertainty, 75; tolerance for, 127
unemployment, 7; and technology, 56
urban forest, 113
urban riots, 89
United States: economic future, 1; economic stability, 3; federal debt, 8; as heterogenous society, 8; illiteracy in, 58; military budget, 17; oil reserves, 68; work force, 29
uranium cost, 69

video games, 54
Volcker, P., 72
volunteer work, 113

war and politics, 74
waste disposal, 101
Water Act, 36
water supplies, 12; pollution of, 12
white-collar workers, productivity of, 55
wildlife extinction, 14
women as priests, 119
wood as fuel, 10, 11
work: attitude toward, 30; and community, 28–31; and perserverance, 134–135
worker dissatisfaction, 30
workers and employer, 30
working hours, 28
working population, 31
work rules, 94
work teams, 30
work week, 28, 29

About the Authors

KENNETH D. WILSON is a management consultant and investment counselor in Southern California. He teaches courses in public policy analysis, organization behavior, and systems management at the University of Southern California, University of California, Los Angeles, and California State University, Long Beach. He is coauthor of *Economic Growth in the Future* (McGraw-Hill 1976), contributing editor of *Prospects for Growth* (Praeger 1978), and coauthor of *Choice over Chance* (Praeger 1981). Dr. Wilson is past president of the Los Angeles chapter of the American Society for Public Administration and member of the World Future Society and the Society for International Development.

RICHARD GOLDHURST is the author of several books on American military history including *Many Are the Hearts: The Agony and Triumph of Ulysses S. Grant*; *Pipe Clay and Drill: John J. Pershing and the American Military Mind*; *The Midnight War: The American Intervention in Russia, 1918–1920*; and *Raid: Patton's Secret Mission.* He is a member of the faculty of Fairfield University in Fairfield, Connecticut and makes his home in Westport, Connecticut.